'This is a rich resource full of references and thoughtful que practice forward to develop p wellbeing for young children. Firmly based on experience, it is full of interventions that really work. I know – I've tried them!'

— *Ruth Fergusson, Senior Educational Psychologist, Brighter Futures CIC*

'In a world of constant change, progress and new ideas and in the ever changing world of education, sometimes we lose sight of the axioms around what young children need to thrive. Through her writings, Sonia clearly states the core elements that make up environments where we can successfully support emotional health and wellbeing. Every early years practitioner should have a dog-eared copy of this book, reminding them of the essential basics that we all need in the promotion of healthy and happy children.'

— *Fred Lacey, play therapist and nurture specialist*

'This important and accessible book is essential reading for professionals working with young children and their parents... The author's ideas about co-adventuring and creativity offer thought-provoking ways to support practice. The chapter devoted to adult wellbeing also addresses a key but often neglected issue – that the adults working with young children need to look after their own health and wellbeing in order to maximise children's health and wellbeing.'

— *Dr Janet Rose, Principal, Norland College*

of related interest

The School of Wellbeing
12 Extraordinary Projects Promoting Children and Young
People's Mental Health and Happiness
Jenny Hulme
ISBN 978 1 78592 096 7
eISBN 978 1 78450 359 8

Positive Body Image for Kids
Ruth MacConville
ISBN 978 1 84905 539 0
eISBN 978 1 78450 047 4

101 Mindful Arts-Based Activities to Get Children and Adolescents Talking
Working with Severe Trauma, Abuse and Neglect Using Found and Everyday Objects
Dawn D'Amico
ISBN 978 1 78592 731 7
eISBN 978 1 78450 422 9

Inspiring and Creative Ideas for Working with Children
How to Build Relationships and Enable Change
Deborah M. Plummer
ISBN 978 1 84905 651 9
eISBN 978 1 78450 146 4

Supporting the Mental Health of Children in Care
Evidence-Based Practice
Edited by Jeune Guishard-Pine OBE,
Gail Coleman-Oluwabusola and Suzanne McCall
Foreword by Jenny Pearce OBE
ISBN 978 1 84905 668 7
eISBN 978 1 78450 172 3

Helping Vulnerable Children and Adolescents to Stay Safe
Creative Ideas and Activities for Building Protective Behaviours
Katie Wrench
Foreword by Ginger Kadlec
ISBN 978 1 84905 676 2
eISBN 978 1 78450 183 9

More Creative Coping Skills for Children
Activities, Games, Stories, and Handouts to Help Children Self-regulate
Bonnie Thomas
ISBN 978 1 78592 021 9
eISBN 978 1 78450 267 6

Promoting Young Children's Emotional Health and Wellbeing

A Practical Guide for Professionals and Parents

Sonia Mainstone-Cotton

Jessica Kingsley *Publishers*
London and Philadelphia

First published in 2017
by Jessica Kingsley Publishers
73 Collier Street
London N1 9BE, UK
and
400 Market Street, Suite 400
Philadelphia, PA 19106, USA

www.jkp.com

Library of Congress Cataloging in Publication Data
A CIP catalog record for this book is available from the Library of Congress

British Library Cataloguing in Publication Data
A CIP catalogue record for this book is available from the British Library

ISBN 978 1 78592 054 7
eISBN 978 1 78450 311 6

Printed and bound in Great Britain

MIX
Paper from
responsible sources
FSC   FSC® C013604

With thanks to
Iain, Lily and Summer for believing in me
Clare, Fred, Louie, Ruth, and to Gwyn and Iain for
reading through the chapters and advising me.

Contents

Introduction

This book focuses on exploring and thinking about emotional health and wellbeing. Every person needs good wellbeing to be able to fully be the person they are meant to be. We often hear about the importance of wellbeing for adults and teenagers; however, we know from research that growing numbers of younger children have low self-esteem and low wellbeing. I believe if we can enable children to have good wellbeing in the early years then we are setting them up with a solid start for their life. This book will be exploring wellbeing and emotional health in young children and offering practical guidance and ideas on how we can promote and increase young children's emotional health and wellbeing.

What is wellbeing?

Wellbeing is a phrase that's often used but it's not always clear what it means. When I started writing this book I asked a group of friends what they think wellbeing is. This group of people included educators, carers, artists, writers, vicars, youth workers. The words they used were: feeling safe, knowing my basic needs are met, knowing I am supported, free to laugh and joke, free to discover my creativity, thriving not surviving, eating a good meal, being able to run.

Words that come to my mind when I think about wellbeing are: feeling loved, feeling safe, loving myself and feeling good about who I am, being able to cope with life's difficulties.

A quick internet search describes wellbeing as: feeling good, functioning well, feeling contented, feeling enjoyment, being resilient. Weare (2015) describes wellbeing as: involving a feeling of happiness, a sense of self worth, having a sense of meaning and purpose to your life, having friendships and relationships which are supportive and understanding, being able to deal with your own emotions.

I believe one of the most important roles we have as adults is to help children to have good wellbeing, and the start of that is helping children to know that they are loved, they are special and they are unique individuals.

Questions for practice and reflection

■ How is your wellbeing?

Look at the words that describe wellbeing, and then take a moment to think about how you feel and think about your emotions around this word.

UNICEF report on wellbeing

In 2007, UNICEF produced a report on the wellbeing of children in 29 countries; Britain was bottom of this league table (UNICEF 2007). This report was a wake-up call to educators, children and youth workers, policy-makers and politicians. The report looked at six different aspects of wellbeing: material wellbeing, education, health and safety, relationships with family and friends, behaviour and risks and children's views of their own wellbeing. Britain got the lowest score in two of these six areas: relationships with family and friends and children's own view of their wellbeing.

The importance of relationships

Part of the measurement for relationships was looking at the number of children who lived in single family households, how many children eat main meals with parents more than once a week, the number of children who said that parents spend time talking and listening to them; and how many children find their peers kind and helpful (UNICEF 2007). This was a clear reminder that wellbeing is not just about what we provide for children but it is also about the importance of the relationships we have with children and the relationships they have with friends. The Children's Society (2009) did further research with children and young people exploring children's views of wellbeing through The Good Childhood Inquiry; they heard evidence from 18,000 children and young people across the UK. Their conclusion from talking with children was that the main things children need for a good wellbeing and to flourish are loving families, friends, a positive lifestyle, good schools, good mental health and enough money (Layard and Dunn 2009). One of the questions the children were asked was: 'What makes for a good family life?' (The Children's Society 2009). Some of the answers included:

'You're there for each other.'

'Respect your family.'

'When trouble comes, you've got to work things out together.'

'A family to love and care about them and to help them with their problems.'

Wellbeing in schools

The National Association of Head Teachers has warned that a fifth of children in school have a mental health problem before the age of 11 (Richardson 2016). Young Minds (2016) report that one in four young people in the UK experience suicidal thoughts. These are alarming statistics, as a society we need to take this seriously. If we can get it right with the early years, by ensuring they have good wellbeing, there is much hope for the future of our children (Weare 2015).

Wellbeing research in early years

People often talk about the wellbeing of adults and teenagers. However, there has been a growing realisation that we need to be talking about the wellbeing of all ages. The London Metropolitan University (LMU) and the National Children's Bureau (NCB) launched a wellbeing project: 'Talking about Young Children's Wellbeing 2009–2011'; the focus was on hearing young children's views on their wellbeing, as well as the views of parents and practitioners (Manning-Morton 2014). Most research on wellbeing has been with older children and many of the ideas that influence policy on wellbeing are based on research with older children The LMU/NCB wellbeing project was a refreshing change, challenging the notion that younger children don't have a view. They showed through their project how children are able to express their ideas about wellbeing. I have worked with early years children for a number of years, finding out their views of wellbeing; in my experience children are keen to share their thoughts and ideas, it needs adults to stop and listen to them.

Wellbeing and views of self

An important aspect of wellbeing is having a positive view of yourself. We know that a growing number of children have poor self-esteem, have poor body images of themselves and feel negative about how they look. In a recent Children's Society report (Pople 2016) they found a third (34%) of girls aged between 10 and 15 years were unhappy about how they look; this figure has risen by four per cent in the last five years. There has also been some recent research by PACEY (2016) that has found 24 per cent of childcare professionals have reported seeing signs that children in their care between the ages of three and five years are unhappy about how they look or unhappy about their body. Pressure on children comes from all kinds of sources, and adults have an important role in helping children to understand and interpret messages about size, appearance and body image. How aware are we of the language we use with children about people's looks, weight, skin colour or clothes? Do we give children praise which focuses on who they are, or how they look? These are important areas to reflect on for any adults spending time with children, but especially for parents and early years professionals.

Questions for practice and reflection

- Think about the children you have worked with recently or your own children. When have you been able to praise them? How often is your praise linked to appearance and how often to behaviour or character?

- Is the praise you give to children the same for both boys and girls? Are there comments you make that are more linked to one gender, e.g. more comments to girls on their appearance?

- Think about comments you make about yourself in front of children. Do you comment on what you like about yourself or are your comments about your body/size/weight negative?

Wellbeing and poverty

We know that poverty has an impact on the wellbeing of children, there is growing evidence and research to show the negative impacts of living in poverty. Living in poverty has a very serious impact on children's mental health and wellbeing. There are recognised links between growing up in poverty and the detrimental effect that can have on educational attainment and health outcomes (Ayre 2016). A research project by The Children's Society with children and young people living in poverty with mental health difficulties found that 'almost a quarter of children don't feel useful compared to 1 in 6 children from more affluent backgrounds' and many children saying that they felt they were failures (Ayre 2016). Recent figures have shown that child poverty is rising; at the end of June 2016 the number of children living in poverty was put at 3.9 million; 66 per cent of these children live in families who are working (Royston 2016). As early years workers and teachers we are seeing a growing effect of poverty on the families we work with and the consequences this brings. There are many nurseries, children's centres and schools who are working hard to support families living in poverty. Several schools I know wash the school uniform of some children, and I know children's centres who sell on clothes, shoes and toys that children have grown out of for very small amounts (e.g. 25p/50p). Other children's centres provide meals for families at lunch time. As budgets are being severely cut to services it is getting harder and harder to provide some of these services, but where they are provided they do help make life a little bit easier for families.

Questions for practice and reflection

- Spend a moment thinking about the children you work with. How is their wellbeing?
- Do you hear children talking negatively about how they look? Do you have a team approach on how you respond to this?

- Do you work with children who are living in poverty? Have you discussed the impact this might be having on the children and their family's wellbeing in staff meetings?
- Are there ways you may be able to help these families who are living in poverty? For example, could you make links to the local food bank, sell on second-hand clothes, etc.?

Wellbeing in the early months and years

Another major factor on the impact of a child's wellbeing is the response of the adults around them. We know through the ongoing development of neuroscience that being loved, nurtured and cared for is essential to a child's wellbeing. Emotionally responsive parenting will develop vital connections in a child's brain which will enable them to deal with stress later in their life. This will help them form loving, caring relationships, deal with anger and frustration and be more resilient (Sunderland 2006). Research has shown that children who are loved and cared for, who have a secure attachment with their caregivers, who have clear boundaries, good language and social development are often the children with good emotional wellbeing (Field 2010). However, it is not just parents who can have a major impact on the development of a child's self-esteem and wellbeing. Other key adults can have a major impact in their lives, including teachers, nursery workers and grandparents, aunts and uncles.

Wellbeing in the early years foundation stage

Promoting the wellbeing of young children is an essential part of the early years foundation stage (EYFS); there is a category in the EYFS (DFES 2007) – personal, social and emotional development (PSED) – dedicated to wellbeing. The guidelines for this recognise the massive impact that good PSED has on children and their wellbeing as they grow and develop into life. The EYFS emphasises the importance of parents and early years practitioners working together to promote children's wellbeing and PSED, highlighting how important all adults are in this role for children.

The role of adults

An important part of increasing wellbeing is having people around us who believe in us, support us, and encourage us. Children need this just as much as adults. Many of the children I work with are fearful of trying new things, they are anxious about having a go; this can lead them to being in a state of panic, rage and fear. The role of the adult is so important in supporting them, gently showing them, guiding them. The role of the adult is to let the child know they believe in them, they will support them and they will guide them.

One of my jobs is as a nurture support worker. I work for a team in Bath called Threeways Brighter Futures;[1] I am part of their Nurture Outreach Service which supports reception-aged children in their transition from pre-school to school, throughout their reception year and across

---

1   www.brighter-futures.uk.net

the transition into Year 1. In this role I spend a lot of time with children who have a low wellbeing, who, for a variety of reasons, are finding life and the transition into school very hard and very scary. This role has taught me so much about the importance of having a good wellbeing. It has also reminded me of the importance of using creative and playful ways of being with children and working with children. This was particularly emphasised to me when I worked with one boy who loved animals. His teacher occasionally brought her old dog into school. We were able to use his love of animals and the dog as a brilliant way to talk about emotions, and he became very good at recognising the dog was happy because she was wagging her tail. Through going on little walks around the school grounds with the boy and the dog, his language developed, he was happier, more engaged and his wellbeing was noticeably growing. There is a growing body of research showing the positive impact animals, particularly dogs, can have on helping people to feel safe and enhancing their wellbeing, particularly people who have experienced trauma (Van Der Kolk 2014).

Development in the brain

Each baby is born with a brain which needs developing. There are cells and pathways which need to be activated; these are activated by how parents respond to, relate to and communicate with their baby. Parents need to sing, talk and read to babies, this will develop and enable good brain development (Rose 2013). Natural chemicals and hormones help to activate these pathways. Oxytocin is naturally released when a baby is born and helps the mother and baby bond. Opioids and oxytocin are chemicals which aid our wellbeing, these chemicals are released when a child or adult is gently touched and lovingly held (Sunderland 2006). These chemicals contribute to us having a good wellbeing, feeling good about ourselves and feeling loved. The opoids and oxytocin that are released when a baby is gently touched are the same in older children, teenagers and adults. Through my nurture work I have really noticed how gently touching a child's arm or stroking their back when they are distressed can really help to calm them down. Kristin Neff (2011) recommends adults using this self soothing on themselves, suggesting that when adults are feeling stressed or unhappy they hold their own arms or stroke their own arm. I recommend trying it – it really helps to bring down stress levels.

Assessment tools for measuring wellbeing in children

For early years settings and schools, Dr Ferre Laevers has created a wellbeing index – there is an excellent YouTube video describing this index and Laevers' work (Laevers 2012). The wellbeing index, called the Leuven involvement scale, is based around observations of the child or a group of children, it has a five point scale to measure the child's wellbeing and involvement. The scale links wellbeing with being resilient, having the confidence to try something new and having a good self-esteem (I discuss this further in Chapter 6).

In my nurture role, our team uses an assessment tool called Thrive (2016); this tool helps us to look at a child's social and emotional development. One of the first stages of the Thrive assessment is looking at a child's 'Being needs': a child needs to feel safe, to feel special and to have their needs met. Initially it is quite easy to look at these criteria and presume that is obvious and something that everyone needs. However, as my colleagues and I have worked with these and reflected on them, I have increasingly realised just how fundamental and vital these are. If a child is feeling scared and unsafe, if they don't believe they are special and don't hear that they are special, if their basic needs are not being met, and this includes the need to be loved, then they cannot be happy, their wellbeing will be low and the way they view and see the world will be through very distorted and unhappy lenses.

Stress

We know that the opposite of good wellbeing is being in a state of stress. Stress can have a serious effect on the body. Long term, high levels of stress can cause many serious health problems, including high blood pressure, heart disease, a weakened immune system and anxiety (Hagan and Nayar 2014). We know that increasing numbers of children are experiencing stress and anxiety, this is sometimes due to feeling under pressure and having limited time to relax and play. I explore in greater detail how we can help children to enjoy moments of quiet, relaxation and times when there is no pressure on them in Chapter 2.

Action for Happiness

A movement has been set up, by experts in the fields of psychology, education and economics, called Action for Happiness;[2] its aim is to create a group of people whose goal is to build a happier and more caring society. They provide ideas and suggestions on how people can take action towards this at home, in work and their communities. They have a toolkit of ideas for school, which is aimed at older children but could be adapted to younger children. I think the ideas behind this movement are really interesting. They link in to the recognition that today we have a society where people are feeling unhappy and stressed and have low wellbeing and that this is not healthy for society.

Negative messages we can carry

When we have poor wellbeing we often have negative stories and beliefs about ourselves. Ian Adams (2016) uses a phrase: 'Belief is stepping into a story that rings true and allowing the story to form you.' Many of the children I work with in my nurture work have a story of themselves that they are stupid, not special, naughty, angry, unloved. I and the educators I work with help these children to have a new story about themselves. One that is about being unique, special, loved, and able. Our role in the year we work with them is to start to change the story they have, to enable them to believe the new story and to begin to live it. We know that the adults in children's lives can have a major impact on the wellbeing of the children they spend time with. Some children we see

---

2   www.actionforhappiness.org

have very hard lives at home, and as adults working with these children we can have a major influence and we can make a real difference. By stopping, listening, taking notice and being nurturing and encouraging, we can begin to raise a child's wellbeing and we can begin to make a difference in their lives.

This rest of this book explores different ways and offers ideas on how we can raise young children's emotional wellbeing. If we can begin to make this happen with the youngest of children, then this will start them off in an excellent way to hopefully becoming resilient and happy children.

Outline of the book

You can read this book either in the whole or as individual chapters. Each chapter works on its own with ideas and suggestions. This book explores seven different topics and ways we can think about children's wellbeing and how we can increase children's wellbeing. Chapter 1 discusses playfulness with outdoor play, looking at how important play is to children's development and how essential the outdoors is to children's wellbeing. Chapter 2 explores how busy our and are children's lives are, it draws on practice from Denmark and looks at the benefits of yoga, mindfulness and daydreaming. In Chapter 3, I consider how we can help children to have a rich emotional literacy and understanding from a young age. Chapter 4 offers ideas and suggestions of how we can use sensory play to enhance children's wellbeing. In Chapter 5, Creativity, I draw on the work from Reggio Emilia; this chapter explores the many different ways we can enable children and ourselves to be creative. Chapter 6 opens up the idea of following children's interests, of adults being able to dance in the moment with children and being able to let go of their own agenda. The final chapter, Chapter 7, is on adult wellbeing, this recognises that if the adults who are caring for children have low wellbeing themselves they are not able to promote the children's wellbeing. This book will give you some ideas and recommendations and it will encourage you to think and reflect on your practice.

References

Adams, I. (2016) *40 Temptations.* London: Proost. Available at www.proost.co.uk/40-temptations, accessed on 19/8/16.

Ayre, D. (2016) *Poor Mental Health: The links between poverty and mental health problems.* Available at www.childrenssociety.org.uk/sites/default/files/poor_mental_health_report.pdf, accessed on 19/8/16.

DFES (2007) *Development Matters in the Early Years Foundation Stage (EYFS).* Available at www.foundationyears.org.uk/files/2012/03/Development-Matters-FINAL-PRINT-AMENDED.pdf, accessed on 10/5/16.

Field, F. (2010) *The Foundation Years: Preventing poor children becoming poor adults.* Available at http://webarchive.nationalarchives.gov.uk/20110120090128/http:/povertyreview.independent.gov.uk/media/20254/poverty-report.pdf, accessed on 29/4/16.

Hagan, I. and Nayar, U. (2014) *Yoga for Children and Young People's Mental Health and Well-being: Research review and reflections on the mental health potentials of yoga.* Available at http://journal.frontiersin.org/article/10.3389/fpsyt.2014.00035/full, accessed on 15/12/16.

Laevers, F. (2012) *Introduction to the Importance of Wellbeing and Involvement.* Available at https://www.youtube.com/watch?v=ArEY-YvbAh, accessed on 19/8/16.

Layard, R. and Dunn, J. (2009) *A Good Childhood: Searching for values in a competitive age.* London: Penguin.

Manning-Morton, J. (2014) *Exploring Wellbeing in the Early Years.* Milton Keynes: Open University Press.

Neff, K. (2011) *Self Compassion.* New York: Harper Collins.

PACEY (2016) 'Children as young as 3 unhappy with their bodies.' Available at https://www.pacey.org.uk/news-and-views/news/children-as-young-as-3-unhappy-with-their-bodies, accessed on 31/8/16.

Pople, L. (2016) *The Good Childhood Report 2016 Summary*. Available at www. childrenssociety.org.uk/what-we-do/research/the-good-childhood-report, accessed on 31/8/16.

Richardson, H. (2016) 'Heads warned over pupils' untreated mental health issues.' Available at www.bbc.co.uk/news/education-35502394, accessed on 1/3/16.

Rose, T. (2013) *Emotional Readiness: How early experiences and mental health predict school success*. North Charleston, SC: Createspace.

Royston, S. (2016) 'Child poverty rises by 200,000 – government must take action.' Available at http://www.endchildpoverty.org.uk/child-poverty-rises-by-200000-government-must-take-action, accessed on 19/8/16.

Sunderland, M. (2006) *What Every Parent Needs to Know*. London: Dorling Kindersley Limited.

The Children's Society (2009) 'The good childhood inquiry: what children told us.' Available at https://www.churchofengland.org/media/39683/1744childrensevidence.pdf, accessed on 11/9/16.

Thrive (2016) www.thriveapproach.co.uk, accessed on 21/2/16.

UNICEF Innocenti Research Centre (2007) 'Child poverty in perspective: An overview of child wellbeing in rich countries, Report Card 7.' Florence: UNICEF Innocenti Research Centre.

Van Der Kolk, B. (2014) *The Body Keeps the Score – Mind, Brain and Body in the Transformation of Trauma*. New York: Penguin.

Weare, K. (2015) 'What works in promoting social and emotional well-being and responding to mental health problems in schools?'Available at www. youngminds.org.uk/assets/0002/2178/NCB__2015__What_works_sociall_emotional_wellbeing_and_mental_health_in_schools.pdf, accessed on 31/10/16.

Young Minds (2016) 'Mental health statistics.' Available at www.youngminds. org.uk/about/whats_the_problem/mental_health_statistics, accessed on 29/10/16.

Chapter 1

Playfulness and Outdoor Play

Learning through play

Play is the main way children learn and discover, it is an important part of a child's emotional, physical, social and cognitive development and is an essential element in a child's wellbeing (Ginsburg 2007). Play is the key way children make sense of the world, how they work through ideas, thoughts, how they practise their newly learnt skills. For children with English as an additional language, play is a crucial way for children to practise their new language (Clark 2015).

There is something wonderful about watching a child learn and develop through their play; they develop the ability to try things again and again until they master a new skill. Play is how children learn about being with others, it helps them to find out what their body can do and it is the way they learn about emotions and how they feel (Bongiorno 2016).

Learning how to play with others

For some children being with others and knowing how to play with others can be really hard; it is a skill they find very difficult, but we know that if they can learn at a young age it provides them with essential life skills. One of the vital roles of the adult in the early years is to support, model and scaffold children's learning in social skills. Children need to be shown how to play alongside others, how to share, how to take turns. These are all vital skills for them to learn before they go to school.

Children's right to play

The importance of a child's right to play has been recognised through Article 31 of the United Nations Convention on the Rights of the Child (UNICEF n.d.). In 1989 Janet Moyles wrote a book emphasising how play is crucial to children learning and discovering the world, and in her latest book she expresses her frustration that early years educators in the UK are still having to fight for the right of children to play and for the recognition of how children learn through play (Moyles 2015).

It is very frustrating that the current Conservative government seems particularly insistent that the way children learn is through being formally educated and appear to be ignoring all the research around children's play and the excellent pedagogical practice from Italy, New Zealand and Scandinavia.

Allowing children to play is essential to their wellbeing, and it is vital that we really understand this.

Developing social wellbeing through play

Play gives children the opportunity to develop their social wellbeing. Through playing with other children they learn how to share, take turns, co-operate and problem solve. Often, through play with other children, they develop their own rules, their own language and it can help to develop resilience (Cole-Hamilton and Gleve 2011).

There are some excellent examples of being able to observe young children playing with others in the Channel 4 documentary *The Secret Life of 4, 5 and 6 Year Olds.* This series gives insight into the language children use when they are playing with others, the social skills they learn, how they make friends and how they cope when things don't go their way. It gives insight into how much children learn through their play and the complexity of what they are learning.

Supporting children's play

Children need a mix of play on their own, play with other children and play with adults; in the very early years, adults are an important play partner. Young children need adults who are able to play and discover alongside them; they need adults who are able to initiate an idea, for example, suggesting 'Let's make a den together', then modelling to the child how to start den making and then allowing the child to let their own imagination and creativity develop the game (Sunderland 2006). A crucial skill for adults is knowing when to stand back in child's play and allow the child to lead and develop, whilst being there showing your interest, curiosity and delight at their play.

An essential element in being a play partner is being curious and open to being delighted. Being able to play with children is an important skill for both parents and educators. I have recently heard several children tell me that adults don't play. This is quite concerning, as this suggests to me that these children are not seeing their caregivers as playful people. In early years settings and reception classes, staff can easily become very focused on completing observations and assessments and setting up for the next activity; these things do need completing but we also need to be playing with the children. Also, parents can be so busy sorting things out in the house that they may miss out on opportunities to play. When we are under pressure we can feel guilty about not playing with our children. I am not wanting to increase that guilt! – but even when we are busy we can still find moments, some spare minutes between doing observations or tidying when we can sit and play. If you can add these moments into your day, this is really valuable to your children.

When adults play with children it is a great opportunity to help scaffold their learning and support them to learn new things (Bruner 1986); it is also a great opportunity to model and encourage language development and social skills. Above all else it is a time to share fun, enjoyment and pleasure. This is something that as adults we need to make time to do, to intentionally set time aside to play with our children and the children we work with.

Questions for practice and reflection

- Spend some time thinking through your day: how many opportunities do you have to play with the children? Do you think this is enough or could you try and play more?
- Can you bring in play into the jobs you need to do, e.g. if you are sweeping up/tidying, do you involve children in this in a playful, fun way?
- Have you asked your children what play they would like to engage in with you?

The play environment

In early years, a lot of attention is given to the environment that children are in. The early years foundation stage (DFES 2007) talks about the enabling environment as needing to be a rich and varied space that supports children's learning and development. Craft (2012) proposes that an enabling learning space is one which enables exploratory play. An enabling environment is a space where children feel safe and relaxed. In the EYFS, the enabling environment is described as the emotional environment, the indoor environment and the outdoor environment (Early Years Matters 2015).

The environment we offer children needs to be an inviting space for children to explore, discover and learn. It needs to be an inviting and attractive environment, which offers children different opportunities. This can be a challenge, especially if we have small spaces. If the space we have is small, for example, if you live in a small flat, there may be a corner of the room which you can make into a play corner, which the child knows is their space. If your setting is in a village hall and you have to pack up at the end of each session, you can still think carefully about how you present the equipment and make it look welcoming and fun to play with. We need to consider how the environment looks and feels, we need to make sure that the environment is not cluttered and that the space limits noise (Early Education 2012). We also need to ensure that the environment encourages communication, language, imagination and creativity. We can do this by thinking carefully about what we are offering, how children can play with the resources, how the play can extend their learning and development and encourage language. We also need to consider carefully how many resources we have out; some settings can look really cluttered with so many different things available. I believe it is better to have less out but for the children to know they can ask for other resources. A cluttered space can make children and staff feel quite stressed.

There are some excellent examples of carefully thought about play environments in Reggio Emilia settings.[1] Reggio Emilia is a northern town in Italy which has developed a creative and reflective ethos to working with children; many early years settings in the UK have been inspired by the thought and beauty that has gone into these spaces (for further discussion, see Chapters 5 and 6). Baby Space in Minneapolis, co-created by Terri Rose, has some really inspiring spaces, carefully designed to meet the differing needs of children and their videos are really worth watching.[2] In the UK, Anna

---

1   www.reggiochildren.it/?lang=en
2   www.babyspace.org/videos.html

Ephgrave (2015) describes and shows pictures in her book of how her school provides a learning environment which enables all children to be engaged in purposeful play of their own choice. These spaces are carefully thought through and created.

Resources we offer

We need to think carefully about the resources we offer to children and ensure we offer open-ended resources. Open-ended resources are resources which children can do many things with, for example, a pop-up tent could be a tent, a rocket, a train or a carwash. Open-ended resources encourage children to use their imagination. This is about allowing children to use their imagination rather than following what the adult requires them to do. We also need to ensure that in nurseries/reception classes the resources are available to children to access themselves. It is not always possible for children to see all of the resources that are available, sometimes room is limited. Ideally you want children to be able to see the resources, for example, on the shelves, in boxes with images on, etc. I know settings where this is not possible, so instead they have made cupboard cards; on the cards are images of the resources available. The children are able to get the card, and show or ask for which toys they want, enabling self selection in a limited space.

Questions for practice and reflection

■ How do children find the things they want in your play space? Are your resources laid out in picture labelled boxes/shelving for them to see?

■ Can children easily move around the play space, does it have open spaces? Or is there a lot of clutter in your play space?

■ Have you got on your knees to see the play space from a child's height? Does the play space look inviting and interesting? Does it work for all the ages in your group?

■ How does the play space encourage children to explore, investigate, discover and ask questions?

■ What range of open-ended resources/toys do you have, for example, pots, pans, containers, blankets to make dens or hide under, toys to push, pull, build with, etc.?

Outdoor play and wellbeing

There is growing evidence to show the important effect spending time in nature and being outside has on children's wellbeing. Recent research has shown that limited access to being outside and nature can have a serious impact on the physical and mental development of children (Strife and Downey 2011).

Spending regular, positive time outside can help children's self-esteem, raise their confidence and develop their physical and mental wellbeing. Being outside can help to enhance children's senses and can help them to develop a connection with the world around them. This is also really relevant for adults. I know myself I feel so much better when I get to spend time outside.

New research has shown that children with attention deficit hyperactivity disorder (ADHD) are calmer and have increased concentration when they spend time outside in nature (Kuo and Faber-Taylor 2004). From my experience, children often know themselves that being outside helps, I have worked with several children who are able to identify that they are becoming stressed/fidgety and anxious and will say, 'I need to get outside to help me calm down.' I worked with one four-year-old who told me, 'When I feel cross I need to go outside and hang upside down, then I feel better.' The setting he was in realised this was important for him and was able to provide this for him.

There is a growing concern in the UK about the lack of outdoor opportunities children have and the negative impact this is having on their wellbeing. Richard Louv (2005) has come up with the phrase 'nature deficit disorder' to describe the negative impact not spending time outdoors can have on people. The Wild Network, an online community which promotes and encourages outdoor play, proposes that we need to promote and allow all children to have lots of opportunities to explore, to be imaginative in the wild, to look and discover and to connect with nature.[3] The outdoors is available to everyone, you don't need to be living in the countryside to access nature, all outdoor spaces, including a balcony, a small patch of grass or a play park, can provide children with a link to nature; as adults we need to help children to access these spaces and experiences (Ward 2008). We have a responsibility to ensure we are not gate keepers, stopping children from accessing the outdoors.

---

3   www.thewildnetwork.com/mission

Very young children have a natural curiosity and desire to explore, but adults can quickly squash this. If we want our children to enjoy being outside and to grow up continuing to be curious and fascinated with what they see, hear and find, then they need adults around them who are also curious, interested and have a desire to explore. As adults, we need to rediscover our own sense of wonder, awe and excitement at being in nature (Louv 2005).

Recently, the National Trust has produced a free resources pack called '50 things to do before you're 11 ¾'.[4] This is a great resource with some lovely ideas and suggestions of fun and free activities to do outside which will enhance your children's wellbeing.

Questions for practice and reflection

- How do you view your outside space? A place to let off steam or a learning environment? (Your outdoor space maybe a nearby park.)
- Spend time observing children in the outdoor space. Watch how the children use the space. What do they play with? How do they play in the space? Do they play with different children when they are outside? Is their play different to when they are inside?
- Do the children who have more challenging behaviour inside behave differently when they are outside?
- How does your outdoor space allow children to be curious about nature?
- How does your own cultural experience impact on being outdoors? For example, if you were told as a child that

---

4   http://nationaltrust.org.uk/50-things-to-do

being outside in the cold would make you catch a cold or you couldn't go out if it was raining, this might affect how you view the outdoors today.

- What do you do when it is raining or very cold? Do you still go outside to play?
- Do you and the children you support have good outdoor clothing, for all weathers?

Using the outdoors to learn

I have observed children being transformed through being outside and playing outside. One child I worked with had limited language: when he was in the classroom he would talk a little but it was limited and very unclear, however, when he was outside his language increased hugely. Often we can miss these developments in children; we need to spend as much time observing children when they are outside as we do when they are inside. Sometimes we can view outdoor play as being an opportunity for children to let off steam, but I have observed some children who appear to learn more and engage more in their learning when they are outside than when they are in.

I live in a small village surrounded by farms. Some of the children in the local schools are farm children and many are children who have experience of being out in the local fields and woods. I have worked with several children who find learning in the classroom very difficult, but their knowledge of the outdoors is amazing, I have learnt from several four- and five-year-olds how to find hen eggs, how to milk cows, the names of birds and where to catch rabbits.

These are children who find traditional learning very hard and often feel that they are stupid and can't do it. I firmly believe if we adjust our ways of teaching children new skills to fit with their interests then they will learn so much more. There was one four-year-old boy who told me that he was already a farmer; he told me about his hens and how he finds their eggs each day; this same little boy also told me how he hated maths, he didn't like numbers and he did not need maths. I knew he was able to count eggs and count his hens. If the school had used real eggs and talked about chickens when they were trying to help him understand numbers, then he may have begun to see that he could already do some maths and realise he didn't need to be scared about it. By thinking creatively about how children learn and how we teach children, we are able to offer them so much more. Sometimes children are held back in their learning by our lack of creative thinking and resourcefulness.

Challenging behaviour

I have had many conversations with staff in early years settings about the challenging behaviour of some of their children, particularly some of their boys. These conversations often start to occur in the spring term before they start school. I often suggest that they need to encourage their children to spend more time outside, they need to provide more opportunities to explore, discover and be physically active outside; I suggest this will often decrease behaviour issues they are having.

Some adults find their children go through a stage of wanting to play a lot of physical, rolling around, rough and tumble play. Staff and parents often find this very difficult to know how to manage. It does need careful watching and managing making sure it doesn't become hurtful; however there is research on the development of the brain that shows rough and tumble play, for example, rolling around on the floor, rolling on top of each other and play fighting, can activate the joy system in a child's brain. This has a natural anti-stress effect on the brain and helps to develop the part of their brain that manages their feelings and emotions (Sunderland 2006). It also helps with developing the central nervous system, which supports children in their development as they grow and develop new skills (Lloyd 2016).

I do believe that being outside is about far more than allowing children to let off steam; we see this model of outdoors so often at playtimes in primary school, but it is not always a good experience and it is a very limited view of outdoor play. Allowing children to have the time to explore, to discover, to investigate outside gives them the opportunity to develop such life-affirming skills. I firmly believe that being outside helps to increase the wellbeing of both children and adults.

Finding out children's views about the outside environment

Often children, particularly young children, want to go outside. Unfortunately, it is not unusual for adults to be less keen. I have worked with many children's centres to help them think about how they listen to children. One children's centre I worked with wanted to find out from children what they thought about their outdoor play area – they asked children to take photos and to film the outdoor space and then asked children about what they liked and disliked. Many of the children told the staff how much they loved being outside, they particularly loved digging in the bark chippings (the one thing the staff were going to get rid of), but they also commented on how sad they felt when their mummies and daddies didn't want to take them outside because it was cold or raining. Another children's centre I worked with recently asked the children from their stay and play session to film their session – when it came to the outside area the children said, 'This is the garden but mummies don't like it in the rain, so we can't play outside when it rains.' Both of these children's centres recognised that they needed to do some work with parents to help them to understand the benefits of outdoor play and how important it is for children to be outside. In an effort to encourage parents to go outside more often, the centres provided wellies and outdoor clothes for both the children and the parents; they also provided information for the parents about why outdoor play was so important and how it helped children's physical and emotional development and wellbeing.

Photo projects with children

I worked on a project in Birmingham to find out the views from children across the city about what made them feel happy, sad and safe in their early years setting.[5] The information was

---

5   See www.childrenssociety.org.uk/what-we-do/helping-children/childrens-society-west-midlands/birmingham-commission-children

being shared with the education team to help inform how they developed their services. For this project, we asked early years settings to get their children to take photos for each category (happy, sad, and safe). The majority of the photos that came back for the happy category involved the outdoor space, with many comments from children such as, 'I feel happy when I am outside,' 'I like playing on the slide,' 'I like looking for bugs.' We also worked on this project with a group of refugee and asylum seeking children living in temporary accommodation; these families were waiting to hear if they had permission to stay in the UK. The children took photos around the building where they were staying and the flats they were living in. The centre had a small play room for them to play in and outside there was a grassy area next to a car park, with rambling roses growing on the side. All the children took photos of the grass area and the flowers; many of these children did not speak English but they were all able to express how much they liked being outside and how much they liked the flowers. One girl told me the pretty flowers made her feel very happy. This was a clear example of the huge difference outdoor spaces, and nature, can make to a child's wellbeing. This child was living in a very stressful environment, living with a lot of uncertainty and fear, and the roses and the outdoor space were helping to give her a moment of finding joy and enhancing her wellbeing.

Asking children to tell us what they like and dislike about their play spaces through using cameras or filming is a wonderful way to see their space/their environment through their eyes. This gives us insight into how the space works for the children. This method of working is inspired by Moss and Clark (2011), the mosaic approach. You can also use this method to involve children in redesigning your play area; it enables you literally to see their play space at their level, through their eyes. Sometimes what you notice is how high the display boards are, how dull the lower spaces – those spaces that are at children's height that we don't notice – are. If you haven't yet tried this with children I would really recommend it.

How to involve children in a photo/filming project of your play space

- I have used cameras with children as young as 18 months (depending on their ability and understanding).

- You can buy children's cameras – these are pretty robust and can be dropped, dropped in water or stepped on (my cameras have experienced all of these and survived). I have also used disposable cameras and cheap digital cameras with children and more recently the camera on an iPad. Using digital cameras enables you to look at the children's work immediately and find out from them what they photographed and why.

- Video recorders are also great to use with children. I use a flip camera; this is a small cheap video camera which is hand held, very easy to use and can be plugged straight into a computer using a USB stick.

- Explain to the children what you want them to do. Show the children how to use the camera or video recorder. Have a conversation with the children about what photos they might like to take.

- You may need to support the children in this project, but it is essential you let the children take the photos they want.

- Once all the photos are taken look at them with the children, find out what they took and why. You could make a book or a display using the photos the children have taken.
- At your next team meeting discuss the photos and what you have learnt from them. Think about what changes you could make based on this information. Then go back to the children and let them know what changes you are going to make from what you learnt from them.

Scandinavian practice

A few years ago I went on a study trip to Denmark. I spent time with a kindergarten whose building was located on the edge of a wood. Each day the staff and children would go for a walk in the woods, usually for between one and two hours. The children were allowed to explore, climb up and over trees, crawl through brambles, pick and eat edible berries. The knowledge the children had of the world around them and their environment was fantastic. The staff had taught them about which foods were safe, how to climb trees, how to take care of their environment. The kindergarten building was full of stuffed animals; these were animals that over the years the children had found, dead, in the woods and then sent to the local taxidermist. So often in the UK we are fearful of talking about death, we often hide dead animals from children, so we don't upset them. What I saw in Denmark was such a contrast to this; there was an acceptance and an acknowledgement about life and death.

Awe and wonder

Another item that I loved at the kindergarten was a cabinet of beautiful found things. I named it their awe and wonder cabinet. In it were things that children had found and valued; it included a dead newt, bird nests, feathers, owl poo. When I returned to the UK I delivered training about the trip to several early years settings and encouraged them to really think about how we use the outdoors with children. There has been a real change over the years in the UK, with a growing realisation of the importance of outdoor provision. As part of the training I took with me my own awe and wonder collection, I now have several – one I use for training, one I have in my own front room and one I have in my small garden office. These include examples of things I and others have found for me. My collection includes an animal skull (I still haven't discovered what it is), large and small crab shells, butterflies, bees, feathers, shells and a wing of a pheasant. When I take these on training days they always create such mixed reactions, some people love them, others are horrified. A question I ask in training is: what do you do when a child brings you a dead bird? How do you respond – with interest and curiosity or with horror?

What I learnt from Denmark is the importance of encouraging and developing the love and curiosity of awe and wonder that children often already have. I firmly believe that developing our awe and wonder is a great way of helping our wellbeing. Young children are often born with a natural curiosity and interest, so often a walk with a two-year-old can take ages as they stop at every leaf, snail and crack in the pavement to explore and discover. As adults, we need to encourage this natural curiosity, but this can be a real challenge when we have such busy schedules for ourselves and for our children.

There is a great piece of film footage about Danish forest kindergartens, 'Kids Gone Wild, Denmark's Forest Kindergartens' (SBS Dateline 2016) – it shows the ethos behind this way of educating children and the positive impact it has on them.

How to create your own awe and wonder collection

- Find a special space to have your collection, e.g. a shelf or a cabinet that can be seen by everyone.

- Explain to the children that this is a special space for things you all find from nature – things that are beautiful, exciting or interesting. Have a conversation about what sort of things you might include. It may be things they find from home or on a holiday.

- Your shelf/space may become full quite quickly! You may need to take stock every few months, have a cull of things and start again, but involve children in this discussion, don't just throw things out without discussing it first.

Forest school

There are a growing number of forest schools in the UK. A few settings are similar in their approach to the Danish model where they spend large chunks of each day outside in the woods. Other settings are not able to offer that much time but do offer one or two sessions a week in a wooded area. A lot of the play that takes place in forest school is child initiated: children are able to take risks (with support), play is often creative and imaginative and is often without the usual time constraints, allowing children space and time to play freely (Knight 2009). An early years podcast with leaders from a forest school in Scotland called Greenbank Woodland Play (2016) is available to hear about how and why their forest school works. It is a useful resource if forest school is a new concept to you.[6]

---

6   http://earlyyears.academy/karen-corrie-greenbank-woodland-play-episode-012

Forest school offers children a very different opportunity to being in a classroom or a garden and for some children it is the first time they have been in a wooded area, the first time they have had the opportunity to balance on a tree trunk or climb a tree. There is much we can learn from the forest school approach. Even if you don't have a wooded area you can use nearby, it is still worth looking at books/websites that advocate the forest school approach. One nursery I worked with was near a beach; forest school didn't work for them but beach school did. They started to regularly take their children to the beach, to play, explore and discover.

Questions for practice and reflection

- Do you have a wooded area or a beach that you can take your children to?
- Is forest school or beach school something that you have considered in your setting? If this is a new idea to you it is worth looking at the Woodland Trust website[7] for ideas and activities you can do outside or Mindstretchers website which has links to resources and videos.[8]

Planning outdoor spaces

As educators and parents, we need to focus as much on the provision we give to children outside as we do inside. Often a large amount of thought, planning and resources go into

---

7   www.woodlandtrust.org.uk
8   www.mindstretchers.co.uk

the indoor classroom, whilst we often we give little time and thought to the outdoor space. Harriman (2006) argues that the belief that learning happens inside is an adult view which stems from adults' need to control rather putting the child's wellbeing first.

The early years foundation stage (DCSF 2007) emphasises the need for the outdoor provision to be offered to all children and suggests it offers children opportunities to use all their senses and to be physically active. An outdoor environment needs to offer children a mix of opportunities. In Chapter 4, I discuss the importance of sensory play – outdoor play can really link with offering children sensory opportunities. For parents or educators who find mess difficult to deal with, giving children the chance to be messy outside can alleviate some of the stress.

Mud kitchens

Several settings I have worked with have recently introduced mud kitchens to their outdoor spaces – this is similar to a kitchen area inside but with mud, water, saucepans, measuring jugs, etc. and children can be creative making lots of potions, cakes, food, etc. Jan White (2012) suggests that mud kitchens are really important for enhancing children's wellbeing and that they provide different opportunities for children to digging in a patch of soil. Her website Muddy Faces provides wonderful examples of the learning and enhancement to a child's wellbeing that mud kitchens can provide, with guidance on how to set up a mud kitchen. I worked with one girl who had high sensory needs, she needed to touch everything and loved covering herself in things like gloop and paint. Her setting introduced a mud kitchen.[9] This girl adored the mud kitchen and she spent a lot of time outside, having her sensory needs met through being able to play in the mud kitchen; this then enabled her to be ready to do the work she needed to do in the classroom.

Ideas for provision in your outdoor space

This is not an exhaustive list, but one to get you started:

- water provision – this could be an outdoor tap, a water tray, half-cut guttering that collects water
- containers to move/carry things – boxes, carts, tubs, buckets, wheelbarrows
- logs, tyres, bricks, sticks
- pots/pans/spoons to make potions, cakes
- netting/tarpaulin for den making
- tools, e.g. spades, brushes, garden forks
- chalks, paint brushes and pots (for mark making with water)
- large boxes to hide in, sit in
- space to run, hide, climb
- bubbles – a simple but always beautiful addition to outdoor play!
- magnifying pots or magnifying lenses to find bugs
- mud or soil
- space to grow things.

---

9   www.muddyfaces.co.uk

Outdoor clothing

To enable children to be able to spend time outside it is essential that they and the adults taking care of them have the right clothing. Many settings encourage parents to bring in wellies, outdoor coats, outdoor trousers; however, I have also worked in many places where parents are unable to do this and the setting provides this for the children. I am a huge advocate of using charity shops and getting parents to pass on clothes and boots that children have grown out of. Not having the right clothing should not be used as an excuse for stopping children accessing the outside.

This can also be an issue for staff; I have been in many settings where the staff don't have adequate outdoor clothing to cope with being outside in all weathers. In the UK, we do have a very different attitude to being outside than our Scandinavian neighbours. On a study tour to Denmark and Sweden I observed how all the staff had the right outdoor clothing; in both these countries, all staff in pre-schools are provided with outdoor clothing as part of their uniform. When I went to Sweden in February, the temperature was around -5°C, but the children and staff spent most of their day outside, playing and exploring; this was possible because they all had the right clothing.

In forest school work there is a saying that there is no such thing as bad weather only bad clothing (Knight 2009). We need to ensure our children get time to be outside every day; having a sheltered area outside can be really useful for when it is very wet.

More questions to help you develop your outdoor space

- Is there space for the children to explore, bushes to look under, natural things to crawl through, spaces to poke, places to hide behind?

- Is there any wildlife in your space? Some children's outdoor spaces are very sterile with so many plastic toys, hardcore flooring, there is no attraction for wildlife.

- How does your space smell? Do you have herbs, flowers?

- How does your space look? Are there things that you need to be down on your knees to see? Are there things you need to look up high to see? Does it look different in each season?

- How does your space feel? Do you have a mix of textures in the garden, e.g. soil, different textured plants, grass, hard services, water, spiky plants.

- How does your space taste? Do you have things in the space that children can taste, e.g. fruit bushes, herbs, vegetables growing?

- How does your outdoor space sound? Are there sounds from birds? Can you hear the wind through twigs or branches (a pot of bamboo is great for this)? Do you have a wind chime or railings that children can make sounds on by running sticks along them?

- Does the space encourage a variety of physical play (that sounds a silly question for outside but I have seen some spaces which are very limited)? Can the children climb, crawl, run, balance, hang upside down, build?

- Are there quiet spaces, e.g. space where children can lie down and gaze at the sky, space where children can stop and just be?

References

Bongiorno, L. (2016) '10 things every parent should know about play.' Available at https://families.naeyc.org/learning-and-development/child-development /10-things-every-parent-should-know-about-play, accessed on 29/10/16.

Bruner, J. (1986) *Actual Minds, Possible Worlds*. Cambridge, MA: Harvard College.

Channel 4 (n.d.) *The Secret Life of 4, 5 and 6 Year Olds*, episode guide. Available at www.channel4.com/programmes/the-secret-life-of-4-5-and-6-year-olds/ episode-guide, accessed on 30/12/15.

Clark, P. (2015) 'Supporting Bilingual Children in the Early Years.' Available at www.naldic.org.uk/eal-teaching-and-learning/outline-guidance/early-years, accessed on 27/05/16.

Cole-Hamilton, I. and Gleave, J. (2011) 'Play and Children's Health and Well-being.' Highlight No. 265. London: National Children's Bureau. Available at www. playpods.co.uk/Images/PlayZine/Ncb%20play%20and%20children's%20 health%20and%20well-being.pdf, accessed on 30/12/15.

Craft, A. (2012) *Creativity, Education and Society*. London: Trentham Books.

Department for Children, Schools and Families (DCSF) (2007) 'Early Years Foundation Stage – child development overview cards.' Available at www. webarchive.nationalarchives.gov.uk/20130401151715/http://www.education. gov.uk/publications/eOrderingDownload/eyfs_cards_0001207.pdf, accessed on 19/12/15.

DFES (2007) *Development Matters in the Early Years Foundation Stage (EYFS)*. Available at www.foundationyears.org.uk/files/2012/03/Development-Matters-FINAL-PRINT-AMENDED.pdf, accessed on 10/5/16.

Early Education (2012) *Development Matters in the Early Years Foundation Stage*. Available at www.foundationyears.org.uk/files/2012/07/Development-Matters-in-the-Early-Years-Foundation-Stage.pdf, accessed on 31/12/15.

Early Years Matters (2015) 'Enabling environments.' Available at www. earlyyearsmatters.co.uk/index.php/eyfs/enabling-environments, accessed on 30/12/15.

Ephgrave, A. (2015) *The Nursery Year in Action*. Abingdon: David Fulton.

Ginsburg, K. (2007) 'The importance of play in promoting healthy child development and maintaining strong parent-child bonds.' Available at http://pediatrics.aappublications.org/content/119/1/182.full, accessed on 19/12/15.

Harriman, H. (2006) *The Outdoor Classroom: A place to learn*. Swindon: Corner to Learn Limited.

Knight, S. (2009) *Forest Schools and Outdoor Learning in the Early Years*. London: Sage.

Kuo, F. and Faber-Taylor, A. (2004) 'A potential natural treatment for attention-deficit/hyperactivity disorder: Evidence from a national study.' Available at www.ncbi.nlm.nih.gov/pmc/articles/PMC1448497, accessed on 19/12/15.

Lloyd, S. (2016) *Improving Sensory Processing in Traumatised Children*. London: Jessica Kingsley Publishers.

Louv, R. (2005) *Last Child in the Woods: Saving our children from nature deficit disorder*. New York: Workman Publishing.

Moss, P. and Clark, A. (2011) *Listening to Young Children: The Mosaic approach*. London: NCB.

Moyles, J. (1989) *Just Playing: The role and status of play in early education*. Milton Keynes: Open University Press.

Moyles, J. (2015) *The Excellence of Play* (4th edition). Milton Keynes: Open University Press.

SBS Dateline (2016) *Kids Gone Wild: Denmark's forest kindergartens*. Available at www.youtube.com/watch?v=Jkiij9dJfcw, accessed on 10/05/16.

Strife, S. and Downey, L. (2011) 'Childhood development and access to nature: A new direction for environmental inequality research.' Available at www.ncbi.nlm.nih.gov/pmc/articles/PMC3162362, accessed on 16/12/15.

Sunderland, M. (2006) *What Every Parent Needs to Know*. London: Dorling Kindersley Limited.

The Children's Society (n.d.) 'The Birmingham Commission for Children: Listening to children in Birmingham.' Available at www.childrenssociety.org.uk/what-we-do/helping-children/childrens-society-west-midlands/birmingham-commission-children/listening-to-children, accessed on 02/01/16.

UNICEF (n.d.) 'Fact Sheet: A summary of the rights under the Convention on the Rights of the Child.' Available at www.unicef.org/crc/files/Rights_overview.pdf, accessed on 19/12/15.

Ward, J. (2008) *I Love Dirt! 52 Activities to Help You and Your Kids Discover the Wonders of Nature*. Boston, MA: Shambhala Publications.

White, J. (2012) 'Making a mud kitchen.' Available at www.muddyfaces.co.uk/infodocs, accessed on 14/12/16.

Chapter 2

Un-rushing and Stillness

We are living in a time where it is accepted as normal to be very busy all the time; it is now almost seen as odd if we are not busy. We fill our own lives and the lives of our children with lots of things to do, places to go, lots of doing and limited slowing down and stopping. Not only is there a huge pressure as adults to be doing all the time, but there is also a pressure on parents to take our children to lots of activities and clubs; this has particularly become a very middle-class issue. And yet we know that being very busy, not slowing down and taking enough rest can be really damaging to our mental and physical health.

Our children have busy lives

There are many children who are living in an environment that is pressurised, busy and rushed (Ginsburg 2007). I knew one six-year-old girl who attended at least one after-school activity every day, sometimes two, and on one day she had three after-school activities in one evening, as well as the activities she did on the weekend. I also know of early years children who attend a language club, ballet lessons, swimming lessons and go to nursery four days a week. The need for filling our children's time can come out of parents' anxiety about their children failing (Williams 2010) or a concern about our children falling behind or missing out on what everyone else is doing. Through this concern and anxiety, we are denying children the opportunity to have times when they can be by themselves and use their own imagination and creativity.

Time to be

There is an argument that children need to have time to be, to have times when they are not being entertained or when they are not in front of a screen. Moments when a child can lie on the grass and gaze at the clouds, times when a child can be curious about what happens when they mix ingredients, times when they are just being. It is at these times that children discover things, find creativity and it can be these times that help a child really develop and discover what they are good at (Purvis 2014) and can enhance their wellbeing. We know that, as adults, being too busy can make us feel stressed, we need to be teaching our children from a young age how to slow down and how to enjoy times of being still and un-rushed.

A child's right to relaxation

The importance of a child's right to relaxation has been recognised through Article 31 of the United Nations Convention on the Rights of the Child (UNICEF n.d.). This article highlights the right all children have to play and relaxation. The article is often quoted as part of a child's right to play, but many miss out the words about a right to relax as well. I think this is a really important part of the legislative act and one that we forget too often. An important question for our practice as early years' workers and also as parents is how much time do we give to our children to relax? Do we fill all their spare time when they are not in school or nursery? Or do we allow them time to just be?

The need for space and exploration in learning

Within the early years foundation stage, under their characteristics of effective learning, there is a recognition of the need to give children space to complete an activity and to explore and have uninterrupted time to play (Early Education 2012). In Reggio Emilia (a northern town in Italy) it is common to see children working on an interest for days, weeks and sometimes months. The staff recognise the importance of allowing children the time and space to try out new ideas, to create and have time to think and problem solve. I explore the Reggio practice more in Chapter 5.

Time for un-rushed and repetitive learning

It appears to me that we now have a socially accepted culture in the UK of being busy; we seem to have forgotten the time it takes to learn new things. We know that children learn from repetition, trying out things, again and again, trying them in a slightly different way, experimenting. We need to allow children un-rushed time to do this. One child I am working with is currently fascinated by ice cubes; each morning in his 1:1 time with his key worker he makes ice cubes, ready for the next day. He has been experimenting with a variety of things to freeze. He takes great delight each day in finding the ice cubes and then melting them. He will often spend 30 minutes plus repeating this activity. His key worker is allowing him the time and space for this child-initiated play, where he is investigating, experimenting, playing and learning in an un-rushed, un-structured, way. This time and space are allowing him to follow an interest, grow in confidence, increase his learning and it is enhancing his wellbeing. His teaching assistant (TA) is supporting his learning and his curiosity, she is scaffolding his learning through his child-led repetitive play.

Children do need their day to have structure and it is particularly important for children with additional needs to know what is happening in a day; visual timetables are great for assisting children with this. However, we can still allow children to go back to their activity after the break for snack/lunch. We don't need to be constantly tidying away all the toys at the end of each session, we could leave them out for the children to return to at a later moment. It is really good to allow children to go back to the same play many, many times, as they learn new things and try out new ideas through this play. I explore this in more detail in Chapter 6.

The space to daydream

Daydreaming, gazing out of the window, is often viewed, particularly in schools, as a negative thing. Daydreaming is often thought of as being lazy and not engaging. I was definitely a daydreamer as a child; I imagined many conversations, stories and scenarios and often engaged in a lot of complicated make-believe play. New evidence shows that daydreaming is vital and an important part of the creative process; children who daydream are often weaving stories in their minds (Dell'Amore 2013).

Researchers have recently found that children who daydream are often the children who are able to play more imaginatively and who are able to make up elaborate stories in their games, which links to them playing for longer and in a more engaged way. They have also found that daydreaming and imaginative make-believe play can help children work through and understand complex emotions and situations (Fries 2009). This would suggest we need to be encouraging children who daydream, but often the opportunity for daydreaming is interrupted by screen time. Ironically, for years people have been concerned that daydreaming stops children from learning, but new evidence is showing that daydreaming is good for children's learning and cognitive development; what we should be concerned about is how screen time is having a negative effect on children's attention span, cognitive development and wellbeing (Brown 2011).

Neuroscientists have shown that for both adults and children, it is when our brain is wandering that we are most creative; it is at those times when we are gazing out, not concentrating, that we can have some of the best creative ideas (May 2012).

Questions for practice and reflection

- What opportunities do the children have in your setting or home to continue their play, their ideas for days, weeks or months?
- Is there space in your setting or home to be able to keep out the den/boat they have made?
- What spaces are there in your setting or home for children to be able to chill out? For example, do you have a cosy corner with bean bags/cushions?

- Do you encourage opportunities to daydream, when children are gazing at the sky or out of the window? Do you recognise these as potential creative moments for a child?
- How much time do you spend daydreaming or having space to not rush?

Danish practice

A few years ago I became really aware that the main conversations I was having with people were about how busy I was, how much work I had to do, how little time I had, how stressed I felt. This awareness came about just before I went on a study trip to a Danish kindergarten. One very noticeable difference in Denmark was how un-rushed their day was. They had their timetable for the day but it was quite loose and flexible, staff would plan around the children and how they were responding each day. If during their daily walk in the woods, children became particularly engaged in some exploration, then they would stay out longer.

I took one photo of a small girl lying on a wooden beam in the setting's garden; she was lying on her back, gazing up at the beautiful blue sky. She stayed there for about 30 minutes, content and peaceful in her own space. This image really resonated with me, and caused me to ask questions: Do we allow children to have time to be un-rushed and still? Do we allow ourselves to be un-rushed and still? The trip to Denmark and particularly the little girl had a really profound impact on my work and my own development. Looking back, I can see how my own interest in wellbeing and my interest in exploring stillness really developed from this trip.

When I came back to the UK I started asking colleagues and others I knew in early years practice about how they help children to find some stillness. Often I had people responding with laughter and comments such as: 'Children don't do stillness,' 'They are on the go all the time.' Some others told me how the children had rest time in the day or a quiet area in which children could sit and read, but often people admitted these spaces were not always used in the intended way. I knew from my own experience of being a parent that it was possible to help children experience stillness. I also knew from events I had run that children can engage in times of quiet. I had experienced young children being able to sit and listen to calming music, while watching beautiful images, in a family meditation experience. I knew from experience that children really benefited from times of calmness. This led me to a search for further information about children and stillness.

Mindfulness

Mindfulness is becoming very popular; there are a number of different books about mindfulness for adults and a growing number about using mindfulness with children. There are courses teaching children mindfulness in schools; in the UK these are mainly aimed at older primary and secondary aged children.[1] Mindfulness uses meditation practice and is also about being aware, living in the moment, noticing and connecting to our self, our body and our breathing and noticing what is around us. Mindfulness is about

1   See, for example, the Mindfulness in Schools project at http://mindfulnessinschools.org/what-is-b

observing what is happening in our body and mind without being critical and encouraging compassion (Williams and Penman 2011). Using mindfulness practice is a great way of nurturing and taking care of ourselves. I believe teaching children mindfulness and helping them to use mindfulness practices is a great life skill for them, which will help them as they grow through life and face difficulties.

Young children are good at living in the moment

In many ways I believe young children are brilliant at living in the moment and noticing. So often taking a walk with a two-year-old can take far longer than the adult intended. Two-year-olds have a natural curiosity, they are great at noticing and stopping; how often do they stop to pick up each stick, smell flowers, peer at a poo, find a snail. They notice the small things, partly because they are shorter and closer to things on the ground, but also because at two years old their brains are wired to notice, to be curious, to discover.

Mindfulness and breathing techniques

Mindfulness practices can help focus on our breathing, there are many mindful exercises using breathing techniques. Mindfulness is often used with older children but I have started to use some of the practices with the younger children I work with. I had one four-year-old child who loved frogs and, inspired by Eline Snel's book (2014). I used some breathing exercises with him, helping him to think about how a frog sits very still and quietly, thinking about how a frog uses slow breathing in and out when he is feeling scared or when he is watching out for flies to eat. I and his TA encouraged him to try breathing like a frog when he was beginning to become agitated and scared.

Using snow globes and sensory bottles to aid breathing

I have also used snow globes and made sensory calming bottles with children,[2] I use these when children are feeling really anxious, stressed and overwhelmed. I acknowledge they seem to be feeling really anxious, we shake the globe or bottle and I get the child to watch the glitter solution as it begins to slow down; at the same time I also ask the child to put their hands on their tummies and notice their breathing; this idea was inspired by Susan Kaiser-Greenland (2010). This is a simple mindful moment, helping the child to notice what is happening in their bodies and helping them to slow their breathing. Afterwards, I then explain to the child how the fizzy feeling in their tummy is like all the whirling around in the snow globe/bottle.

Rocking stuffed toys with our breath

Susan Kaiser-Greenland (2010) suggests a breathing exercise with young children using a stuffed toy. She encourages children to lie on the floor and imagine they are a starfish, stretching all their limbs; she then places a stuffed toy on their tummy and gets the children to rock the toy to sleep through breathing in and breathing out and focusing on

---

2   There are some brilliant ideas if you search for sensory calming bottles on Pinterest.

their breathing. I have used this exercise with a couple of four-year-olds. At first, they found it very funny and were a bit unsure, but by repeating this exercise they became more familiar with it. These are very simple and effective ways to begin to introduce children to mindful practices and focusing on their breathing.

Using bubbles and breathing

Some children (and adults) find it very difficult to focus on their breathing. I have found using bubbles can help to introduce deep breathing techniques. Get the child to take a breath and then slowly blow out through the bubble wand; doing this exercise will slow their breathing. Often when we are stressed or anxious our breathing quickens, this is the same with children. If we exhale for longer than we inhale, this slows down our breathing, reduces our heart rate and can help to bring some calmness. With older children you can introduce a breathing exercise called 7/11 breathing: breathe in for the count of 7 and breathe out for the count of 11. With younger children this is too complex, but from around age three or four, they can blow out for bubbles.

Using mindfulness with children can help develop their curiosity, it can aid children in calming down, by recognising what is happening in their bodies and with their breathing. Using mindfulness can help children to stop judging themselves and to become more self-compassionate (Kaiser-Greenland 2010). These all contribute to a child's healthy emotional wellbeing.

Yoga with children

Yoga practice with children and teenagers has been really growing over the last decade. There is excellent research to show that introducing yoga practice in schools is helping to develop children's resilience and helping them regulate their feelings and emotions (Hagan and Nayar 2014). A friend of mine has been teaching yoga to children and young people for a long time. She describes how at the start of each yoga session she asks the individuals in the group how they feel. She has found many of the children and young people comment that it is the first time that week someone has asked them how they feel. She has recently set up a charity called TeenYoga, training adults to teach yoga to teenagers.[3]

Yoga with children in the early years often uses stories and children's songs, to help the children to be physical and to be in touch with their bodies. I have another friend who teaches yoga to nursery children; she uses stories such as *Dear Zoo* (Campbell 2010) to teach children some of the yoga postures, for example dog poses. Through using familiar stories and songs, you are able to help children learn some yoga positions and also begin to focus on their breathing and what is happening in their bodies. Using movement helps children to release all the fizziness in their body, then at the end of the sessions, they use a short stillness/mindful exercise where the children lie on their backs and listen to some music or calming words and focus on their breathing. The combination of the movement and then the stopping and stillness works extremely well with children of

---

3   www.teenyoga.co.uk

all ages. There are many good books available for teaching children some yoga positions and practice. I have used *My Daddy is a Pretzel: Yoga for Parents and Kids* (Baptise 2012) with younger children; he uses a lovely simple story and instructions on a variety of yoga postures. There are also many yoga apps that have video instructions which you can download onto a tablet.

Using stories to help children find stillness

Reading to children is also an excellent way to help bring a time of stillness and calmness. Many primary schools read a story at the end of the day as a way to help children to relax at the end of a busy day. One reception class teacher I work with has started using Relax Kids (Viegas 2015) stories: short fairytale stories with a short meditation entwined into the story to help all the children find some calmness. You don't need specially written mindful stories; reading books to children can be a wonderful way to help them find some stillness. For generations, reading to children before bedtime as part of daily routine has been an important way of helping children to relax and calm down before they go to sleep. Helping children learn how to find some stillness and calmness is an essential part of enhancing their wellbeing.

Questions for practice and reflection

■ Do you have times in the day with children when you use calmness techniques?

■ There are many yoga teachers who teach early years and primary aged children; consider if this is something you could introduce to your setting.

■ What practices do you use to calm yourself? Have you considered using mindfulness? There are many courses that teach adults mindfulness and many books that help explain the mindful practice. One of my favourite introduction to mindfulness books is by Mark Williams and Dr Danny Penman (2011).

References

Baptise, B. (2012) *My Daddy is a Pretzel: Yoga for Parents and Kids*. Bath: Barefoot Books.

Brown, A. (2011) 'Media use by children younger than two years.' Available at http://pediatrics.aappublications.org/content/128/5/1040.full, accessed on 06/03/16.

Campbell, R. (2010) *Dear Zoo*. London: Macmilllan.

Dell'Amore, C. (2013) 'Five surprising facts about daydreaming.' *National Geographic*, July 16. Available at http://news.nationalgeographic.com/news/2013/07/130716-daydreaming-science-health-brain, accessed on 29/10/16.

Early Education (2012) 'Development Matters in the Early Years Foundation Stage.' Available at www.foundationyears.org.uk/files/2012/07/Development-Matters-in-the-Early-Years-Foundation-Stage.pdf, accessed on 31/12/15.

Fries, A. (2009) 'How daydreaming helps children process information and explore ideas.' Available at www.psychologytoday.com/blog/the-power-daydreaming/200910/how-daydreaming-helps-children-process-information-and-explore, accessed on 06/03/16.

Ginsburg, K. (2007) 'The importance of play in promoting healthy child development and maintaining strong parent–child bonds.' Available at http://pediatrics.aappublications.org/content/119/1/182.full, accessed on 19/12/15.

Hagan, I. and Nayar, U. (2014) *Yoga for Children and Young People's Mental Health and Well-being: Research review and reflections on the mental health potentials of yoga.* Available at http://journal.frontiersin.org/article/10.3389/fpsyt.2014.00035/full, accessed on 15/12/16.

Kaiser-Greenland, S. (2010) *The Mindful Child.* New York: Free Press.

May, M. (2012) 'The neuroscience of creativity: Why daydreaming matters.' Available at www.americanexpress.com/us/small-business/openforum/articles/the-neuroscience-of-creativity-why-daydreaming-matters, accessed on 13/03/16.

Purvis, L. (2014) 'Boredom is every child's human right. It is the fount of creativity.' *The Telegraph,* April 14. Available at www.telegraph.co.uk/news/health/children/10775629/Boredom-is-every-childs-human-right.-It-is-the-fount-of-creativity.html, accessed on 21/02/16.

Snel, E. (2014) *Sitting like a Frog – Mindfulness Exercises for Kids and their Parents.* London: Shambhala.

UNICEF (n.d.) 'Fact Sheet: A summary of the rights under the Convention on the Rights of the Child.' Available at www.unicef.org/crc/files/Rights_overview.pdf, accessed on 19/12/15.

Viegas, M. (2015) *Relax Kids – Aladdin's Magic Carpet: Let Snow White, the Wizard of Oz and Other Fairytale Characters Show You and Your Child How to Meditate and Relax.* London: Our Street Books.

Williams, M. and Penman, D. (2011) *Mindfulness: A Practical Guide to Finding Peace in a Frantic World.* London: Piatkus.

Williams, R. (2010) 'Middle class children are too busy, says head.' *The Guardian,* 21 February. Available at www.theguardian.com/education/2010/may/12/middle-class-children-too-busy, accessed on 21/02/2016.

Chapter 3

Emotional Vocabulary

Helping children to grow in their emotional vocabulary and understanding
Emotional intelligence

An emotional vocabulary and good emotional intelligence are vital for our wellbeing. Understanding what we are feeling, why we are feeling that way, and how we are responding to those feelings is an essential part of understanding ourselves. Having emotional intelligence is vital for ourselves but also crucial in helping us to be with and understand other people. Emotional intelligence helps us to understand our emotions and feelings and how to manage them.

Difficulties when emotional intelligence is low

At the far end of the scale, we see examples of the harm caused when people don't have good emotional intelligence and understanding. Studies that have looked at prisoners' emotional intelligence have found alarmingly high rates of prisoners having a lower emotional intelligence compared to the majority of people not in the prison system. The study found links between low emotional intelligence, impulsivity, aggression and offending (Sharma, Prakash and Singh 2015).

Embedding emotional intelligence in our work with children

It is essential that we teach children an emotional vocabulary and enable them to have healthy emotional intelligence from a young age. A key part of my nurture work with four-year-olds is helping them to learn an emotional vocabulary. It is vital that we help children to learn about feelings and emotions and what these feel like in our body, from a young age.

Some nurseries spend time each day in circle time with their older children, using simple images of emotions/faces and asking children how they feel that day. I know another nursery where the staff ask their pre-school children to self-register each morning by putting their photo on an emotion picture each day. The staff then look at the photos, take note of how the children are feeling and talk to the children about it, sometimes just a comment such as, 'Lucy I see you are feeling happy today, that is great, what is making you happy today,' or 'Sam, I am sorry to see you are feeling sad today, do you want to talk to me about it?' By regularly talking to children about their emotions and how this makes them feel inside, we are helping children to understand what is happening in their heads and how this makes their body feel.

Another nursery spends time with their pre-school children in circle time talking about how they feel that day and how that makes them feel inside their body; adults model this by saying, 'I am feeling very happy and excited today, my tummy feels all fluttery and bouncy,' or 'I am feeling a bit worried today, my tummy is feeling a bit racing and my breathing is going a bit fast.' Understanding our emotions and feelings and what these are doing to our body, and having the language to describe this is a vital skill we can pass on to children.

An alternative school in Bath called The Green House Project has emotional intelligence and the wellbeing of their children as a foundation underpinning their ethos and practice. Each morning they spend time in circle time; they start by asking the children how they are feeling that day, either by children giving a number or showing on their fingers. They then ask the children to name their feelings, encouraging and supporting them to use a rich vocabulary; if a child shows a low number they ask the child what help they need from the group that day. Through this practice, they are acknowledging and validating children's feelings and emotions. They are teaching children from a young age that feelings and emotions are not wrong or bad and the importance of recognising how we feel.

Emotional intelligence as a foundation of learning

In Scandinavian countries, children don't start school until they are six or seven. The children attend kindergartens before this age. Staff in the kindergartens I visited in both Denmark and Sweden informed me that the emphasis before the children go to school is on teaching them social and emotional skills. They believe that this foundational learning needs to be in place before they are ready to begin with more academic learning. Bruce (2010) suggests a child needs to feel safe and secure emotionally before they are ready to learn. This is worth stopping and thinking about.

Questions for practice and reflection

- How many children in your setting are finding it very hard to learn?
- Are those children feeling safe and secure emotionally?
- What are you doing to help them feel more safe and secure?

Social and Emotional Aspects of Learning (SEAL)

In 2005, the government (DFE) produced resources for primary schools called Social and Emotional Aspects of Learning (SEAL). SEAL was used across the primary curriculum and some settings adapted the resources for their nurseries and reception classes. These resources helped schools to explore with whole classes and whole schools an emotional vocabulary and understanding; the aim was to raise children's emotional intelligence. There were many good things about this resource, particularly as it enabled schools to use it as a whole school and whole class approach. Sadly this resource appears to be rarely used now. I know of a few teachers who still use it but they are in the minority. When you look for the resource online it is now under government archived material.

Teaching emotional intelligence in schools

I have observed recently that regular teaching and learning about emotional understanding and intelligence is missing from many UK primary schools. I believe this is partly due to the increasing pressure from government to ensure all children are reaching high levels of academic attainment; also schools have more targets to reach, more things they need to achieve. Many teachers have commented to me how hard it is to 'fit everything in' now. Because of this, many schools feel they don't have the time to focus on social and emotional skills. In some schools, social and emotional learning seems to have been dropped completely.

Focus on targeted groups

I often observe social and emotional work being covered in small group work, with targeted children who have been identified as needing additional support in this area. Sometimes I see it covered as short topic work in personal, social and health education (PSHE) lessons. It is good to offer targeted work with small groups of children; however I do feel there is a huge benefit in the subject being focused on regularly, throughout the year, for all the children in the class/school. All children would benefit from this.

Whole setting approach

Anthony Seldon (2015) actively promoted the teaching of happiness, self-awareness and emotional intelligence across his school when he was headteacher at Wellington College, an independent co-educational secondary school in England (there is an argument this it is easier for private schools as they are under less scrutiny and pressure from government). A recent government study looking at the effectiveness of teaching personal, social and emotional skills in the state schools in the UK found that teaching was most effective when it was delivered as both a whole school approach and with targeted groups; they suggested it needed to be an embedded approach. They also found good evidence to show the positive impact this could have on children and young people (Clarke *et al.* 2015).

Learning from America

Daniel Goleman (1996) wrote about schools in America which were teaching emotional intelligence across ages, including in high schools. These lessons were teaching children about self-awareness, feelings, emotions, and building an emotional vocabulary. These schools' belief was this was essential for every child, not just the children who were identified with extra needs. They found issues with problem behaviour in the schools decreased, pupils had increased attention, pupils had an increase in empathy and understanding others' feelings, pupils were better at problem solving in relationships and it improved children's academic achievement. The pupils had an increased ability to be able to concentrate, focus on their work and cared about their learning.

Embedding it into our daily practice

Professor Weare (2015) has published a paper advising schools in the UK on how to promote wellbeing in schools.

They recommend a whole school approach, which is integrated across the school with pupils and staff. They suggest that it is vital for senior leaders who are leading on this to fully understand it. This is not only relevant to schools but is also relevant to early years. It is essential that leaders fully understand the importance of promoting wellbeing and emotional intelligence. Leaders need to lead by example, by ensuring that they promote wellbeing in their staff and think about their own wellbeing. I will explore this more in Chapter 7. If we expect staff to lead on teaching social intelligence and actively promoting and focusing on teaching social and emotional skills, then we need to ensure that staff are trained, supported and given the right tools and resources for this.

Getting it right in the early years

It is recognised that early identification of low wellbeing and offering early support in the early years and in reception classes can prevent later mental health problems (Weare 2015). In early years, we are in an excellent position to get it right. One of the prime areas of learning in the EYFS (Early Education 2012) is personal, social and emotional development, and the categories which make this up are making relationships, self-confidence and self-awareness, and managing feelings and behaviour. The EYFS proposes that from 16 to 26 months we begin to help young children name and label their emotions, that we do this by acknowledging and talking to them about what they are feeling. They also suggest that adults are modelling and naming their own feelings, for example, 'I am feeling a bit sad now because the toy is broken.' If we really integrate the personal, social and emotional development guidelines into our practice then we are giving children the best start.

The key person approach

The key person approach is an essential and integral element in the EYFS, recognising the need for children to build close relationships and attachment with a key adult to help them feel safe and secure. We know that, for children in nurseries and childcare, if the child builds a strong secure attachment with nursery staff it helps them to feel that they are special, they are wanted, valuable and loveable; this will help them to go on and develop strong relationships in the future (Elfer, Goldschmied and Selleck 2003). As early years staff, we need to feel confident and comfortable about telling the children we work with how special they are and how much we care about them.

Questions for practice and reflection

- When was the last time your staff team took time out to focus on how you implement the personal, social and emotional development in the EYFS?
- How often do you have regular conversations with colleagues and take time to reflect on your own understanding of emotional intelligence?
- How confident do you feel in using emotional vocabulary and recognising how you are feeling? If you are a parent, are you using emotional vocabulary with your children?

Resources to use with early years children

There are a growing number of resources to use with young children that help them to understand their emotions and feelings. Pinterest has a variety of free resources that people can download, including facial images of emotions. Examples of ones I use are emotion bingo, emotion snap, misfit emotions. While playing the game the children need to name and identify the emotion on the picture; they love playing the games and it is also a good way of teaching turn taking. I also regularly make wooden spoon puppets with the children, using a variety of materials such as velvet, cord, silk, google eyes, pipe cleaners, small shape stickers, wool and string. The children can design their spoon puppet to have whichever emotion they want; we talk about what the puppet is feeling and what might have made them feel like that. I also use a lot of mirror games, playing a game which gets children to take it in turns with me to show an emotion face in the mirror. I have also made emotion nature pictures, using flowers, leaves, sticks to make pictures of faces and different feelings. These are all fun and simple ways to help children develop an emotional vocabulary and understanding.

Films covering emotions

In 2015, two excellent children's films with a focus on emotions were released: *Inside Out* and *Song of the Sea*. I think both films are excellent; *Song of the Sea* is less well known, but is really worth watching and sharing with children. Both films recognise feelings and emotions. I have used the *Inside Out* characters in some of my nurture work, particularly because this is a more familiar Disney film, and so recognised by more children. I have *Inside Out* small dolls which I often use to help children explore and talk about feelings and emotions. The children I work with love these characters, particularly the angry character; they often use them in their imaginative play.

Books

I also use books a lot, as they are a wonderful way to explore different feelings and emotions with children. A few of the ones I use regularly are *How are You Feeling Today* by Molly Potter (2014), *All Kinds of Feelings* by Emma Brownjohn (2003), *The Great Big Book of Feelings* by Mary Hoffman and Ros Asquith (2016), *My Many Coloured Days* by Dr Seuss (1973) and also *The Huge Bag of Worries* by Virginia Ironside (2011) with slightly older children (aged 4+).

Apps

There are also a growing number of apps available for tablets and phones which explore emotions. I have mixed feelings about using screen devices with young children, but for short periods of time and whilst being used with an adult, they can be useful. Some of the ones I like are Touch and Learn Emotions by Innovative Mobile Apps, Emotions and Feelings by Joe Scrivens and Montessori Family and Feelings by Pratik Machchar.

Suggestions for embedding emotional intelligence into daily practice

- Use the words of emotion in your daily practice, e.g. 'I can see you are crying because Mummy has gone home, I think that is making you feel really sad, it's ok to feel sad. Mummy will be back after lunch.'

- Help children to understand their feelings: 'You look really happy playing with the train, you have a big smile on your face and you're laughing.'

- Use mirrors to help show children what emotions look like. Play games with the mirrors showing happy faces/sad faces/angry faces/surprised faces, etc. Model to the child what they look like. As the children get older and their emotional vocabulary extends, have fun in trying out more complex emotions and language, e.g. scared.

- With children aged three plus use circle time to explore how they are feeling, talk about feelings, get children to use pictures of emotions to show what they are feeling at that moment.

- Across the ages use story books which explore emotions.

- With children aged three plus use puppets to explore emotions, e.g. how the puppet is feeling, what has made the puppet sad?

- Think about how you encourage your staff and yourself to be open and emotionally self-aware.

- In supervision, ensure you are checking with your staff how they are feeling.

Carers' emotional response to babies and young children

The way we parent and care for babies and young children has a major effect on how children's brains develop, how resilient they are and how they have a good wellbeing. If as adults we respond to children in an emotionally responsive way then we will enable connections to be made which will help develop their brain; this will help children to cope with stress later on in life (Sunderland 2006). To be able to do this, adults need to be mindful and aware of the way they are responding to a baby or young child's emotions. Babies learn from how adults respond to their emotions and distress; as adults we can help babies learn how to go from distress and upset to comfort and calmness. If we ignore babies' emotional needs they don't learn how to be soothed, and if we respond with anger to an upset baby they can become passive and withdrawn (Gottman and Declaire 1997). By appropriately responding to a baby, through calming words, rocking and calming sounds, we are beginning to help to teach a baby to self-soothe and to not be afraid of their strong emotions. This requires a mindful response from the adults, being aware of the baby's emotions and also our own and being mindful of how we are responding. This is not just about parents but also other people who care for our young children, for example childminders, nursery workers, grandparents. When babies learn to be calmed and begin to learn to calm themselves, for example through thumb sucking or stroking a blanket, they are developing vital skills they will need as they grow older. As a child learns to be calm and to focus their attention, this will aid their concentration as they get older (Gottman and Declaire 1997).

Emotion coaching

Emotion coaching is a new approach, which is gaining recognition. This idea is based on work by John Gottman and his colleagues (Gottman and Declaire 1997). Emotion coaching is about emotional regulation; this is in contrast to other forms of parenting or child management styles which are often based on behaviour modification (Rose, Gilbert and Richards 2016). The emphasis with emotion coaching is to aid a child in understanding the emotions they are experiencing and feeling. This is by acknowledging and naming how the child is feeling. It is about validating how a child feels, not dismissing it, and then helping to find a way forward and a strategy to deal with the problem. Emotion coaching enables the adults to teach children about their feelings and emotions.

Often as adults, we can find children's strong emotions and feelings very difficult to respond to. Sometimes children's strong feelings can make us feel uncomfortable. I have often seen practitioners deal with a very distraught child when their mum has left, by trying to distract them, not commenting on their distress or telling them to stop. Another way to deal with this, using an emotion coaching approach, is to acknowledge the child's strong feelings, for example, 'Lucy I can see you are very upset and tearful because Mummy has gone, I think you are feeling really sad because Mummy is not here. That's ok to feel sad, but Mummy is coming back later. Let's sit here and have a cuddle while you are feeling sad and then when you are ready we can go and play.' By using this emotion language you are helping the child to understand their strong feelings, to feel accepted, to name their feelings and to know they are not on their own during this hard time and you are helping to soothe them in an appropriate way.

Emotion coaching is a very valuable tool; it helps adults to rethink how they view children's behaviour. All behaviour is a form of communication and emotion coaching helps adults to view and understand the feelings that are behind the behaviour. Using emotion coaching helps children to understand their emotions, they are being encouraged to name their emotions and they are being supported to find ways to deal with their emotions (Rose *et al.* 2016). Emotion coaching is not a woolly parenting style. Through emotion coaching you also use clear boundaries with the children, making it clear if their behaviour is not acceptable, but it is also recognising the feelings behind the behaviour, for example, 'Poppy, I am wondering if you are feeling really cross right now because Peter has your toy cat, you are frowning and stamping your feet. But it is not ok to hit Peter, we do not hit people. Look Peter is crying, his face is really sad, this is because you hit him. We need to think about what else we can do if you are feeling cross with Peter, can you talk to me about it?' The clear message you are giving is that you understand the feeling but the behaviour is not acceptable. Rose *et al.* (2016) propose there are three main steps to use in emotion coaching:

- Step 1 – Recognising, empathising, validating and labelling feelings

- Step 2 – Limit setting

- Step 3 – Problem-solving.

Research has shown using emotion coaching and raising a child's emotional intelligence enables children to relate better to other children, to concentrate more, to calm themselves more effectively and to deal appropriately with conflict (Gottman and Declaire 1997). By using emotion coaching we are setting our children up to have a good emotional intelligence and understanding.

Questions for practice and reflection

- How do you or your staff manage children's strong emotions? Do you acknowledge them or do you try to distract them?
- Can you think of times and situations when emotion coaching could work well in your setting?
- Is this an area in which your staff need some training and development?

References

Brownjohn, E. (2003) *All Kinds of Feelings*. London: Tango Books.

Bruce, C. (2010) *Emotional Literacy in the Early Years*. London: Sage.

Clarke, A., Morreale, S., Field, C-A., Hussein,Y. and Barry, M. (2015) 'What works in enhancing social and emotional skills development during childhood and adolescence?' Available at www.eif.org.uk/wp-content/uploads/2015/03/Review-of-Social-and-Emotional-Skills-Based-Intervention_Report-WEB-VERSION.pdf, accessed on 07/04/16.

DFE (2005) 'Social and Emotional Aspects of Learning (SEAL): Improving behaviour, improving learning.' Available at http://webarchive.nationalarchives.gov.uk/20110809101133/nsonline.org.uk/node/87009, accessed on 30/03/16.

Dr Seuss (1973) *My Many Coloured Days*. London: Redfox, Random House Group.

Early Education (2012) 'Development Matters in the Early Years Foundation Stage.' Available at www.foundationyears.org.uk/files/2012/07/Development-Matters-in-the-Early-Years-Foundation-Stage.pdf, accessed on 31/12/15.

Elfer, P., Goldschmied, E. and Selleck, D. (2003) *Key Person in the Nursery: Building Relationships for Quality Provision*. Abingdon: David Fulton Publishers.

Goleman, D. (1996) *Emotional Intelligence: Why It Can Matter More Than IQ*. London: Bloomsbury.

Gottman, J. and Declaire, J. (1997) *The Heart of Parenting: How to Raise an Emotionally Intelligent Child*. London: Bloomsbury.

Hoffman, M. and Asquith, R. (2016) *The Great Big Book of Feelings*. London: Frances Lincoln Children's Books.

Ironside, V. (2011) *The Huge Bag of Worries*. London: Hodder Children's Books.

Potter, M. (2014) *How are You Feeling Today?* London: Featherstone Education.

Rose, J., Gilbert, L. and Richards, V. (2016) *Health and Wellbeing in Early Childhood*. London: Sage.

Seldon, A. (2015) *Beyond Happiness*. London: Hodder and Stoughton.

Sharma, N., Prakash. O., Sewgar, K.S., Choudhury, S. and Singh, A. (2015) 'The relation between emotional intelligence and criminal behaviour: A study among convicted criminals.' Available at www.ncbi.nlm.nih.gov/pmc/articles/PMC4525433, accessed on 30/3/16.

Sunderland, M. (2006) *What Every Parent Needs to Know*. London: Dorling Kindersley.

Weare, K. (2015) 'What works in promoting social and emotional well-being and responding to mental health problems in schools?'Available at www.youngminds.org.uk/assets/0002/2178/NCB__2015__What_works_sociall_emotional_wellbeing_and_mental_health_in_schools.pdf, accessed on 31/10/16.

Chapter 4

Sensory Play

Sensory play, sometimes known as messy play, is an essential element in a child's early learning and an essential part of helping their wellbeing. Sensory play is simply play that uses one or more of the senses (Gascoyne 2013); you could argue that all play does this, but I see sensory play as an active engagement of the senses.

We know that children learn through experimenting, through their senses, through their touching, hearing, seeing and tasting. Babies start engaging in sensory play and learning through the way they explore their food with their hands (Beckerleg 2009). Think about mealtimes with a baby who is just being offered food – they automatically put their hands in the food, smear it over their faces, it often goes everywhere. This is young children engaging and learning through their senses, it is the beginning of their learning journey, using all their senses to discover the world around them.

Through stimulating their senses children begin to strengthen the neural pathways in their brain, which helps in future learning (Gainsley 2011). The neural pathways in the brain pass around information about what we are tasting, seeing, hearing, smelling and touching, as well as how it makes us feel, if we like it, dislike it, or find it disgusting (Gascoyne 2013). The opportunity for young children to develop these experiences is a vital start to their learning and development.

Sensory play is about the doing, the exploring, the trying out, the experimenting. It is very hard to explain to a child how ice feels through using words or pictures, but give a child some ice to feel, touch and watch melt, then they begin to understand what the word 'freezing' means. From this hands-on experience, they can then relate to shivering, feeling really cold and begin to understand what frozen is and means. Sensory play is about the experience, it is not about making a beautiful finished project, you mostly don't have anything to show for it at the end, other than some cleaning up!! Sensory play can be a wonderfully liberating and free form of play. Often children will play for extended periods of time with sensory play, they learn so much through this hands-on, experiential form of learning.

Sensory play in the home

I have worked in early years for over 25 years; over that time I have noticed a decline in how many parents are willing to allow their children to do sensory play at home. This can be for many reasons – it may be the thought of tidying up and cleaning up the mess is too depressing, or the lack of room in the house. I am a huge advocate of sensory play and will always encourage parents with young children to try it. It doesn't always have to be really messy, there are many different ways a child can explore and experience sensory play without a huge amount of mess.

Nurseries and children's centres are often very good at providing sensory play opportunities, but this is something that sometimes falls away in reception classes and certainly is rarely done with older children. It probably won't surprise you to hear that my own children had lots of opportunities to do sensory play at home, in one half term holiday when my youngest child was in Year 1 and my eldest was in Year 3, my youngest said she wanted to do bubble painting as, in her words, they didn't do fun things like that at school anymore. So we set up bubble painting in our dining room. This was inevitably very messy, the bubbles oozed over the pot, the girls took great delight in catching them with the paper, this activity soon developed into hand painting, then foot painting; we eventually ended up putting a long piece of paper through the kitchen, into the dining room, with a tray of paint at one end and a bowl of water at the other. In the end, this activity turned into full body painting, the girls found it particularly funny to do bottom prints. I often use this story in training and I usually have a mix of responses. Some people in the room will be delighted and nod and smile in agreement at the importance of sensory play across the ages; others will hear it and shake their heads and look horrified and ask, 'Did you really do that in your kitchen and dining room?'

Sensory play and attachment

Sensory play is also a wonderful way to build on the attachment between the carer and the child, particularly when playing things such as massaging baby lotion into hands and doing hand prints, or playing together and laughing and chasing bubbles. These relaxed and un-rushed experiences can bring deep moments of togetherness, a shared enjoyable experience and moments of joy. These moments are wonderful for both the child and parent and can provide a release of dopamine and opioid chemicals in the brain. These chemicals help people to feel hope and resilience, and increase their wellbeing (Sunderland 2006).

Using play dough

Sensory play at home can be as simple as using play dough, either pots you have bought or that you have made at home. Play dough is widely available now to buy, many supermarkets and toy shops sell it cheaply. It is also very simple and cheap to make. Last year I discovered Pinterest, this has so many ideas and recipes for play dough. One of my favourite projects this year has been making cloud dough, using corn flour and cheap hair conditioner; it smells beautiful and has a very curious soft and crumbly texture. Another favourite has been making play dough with lavender from my garden added to it, this has a very calming effect on children and staff! I have added one recipe here, but there are so many different ones, I would encourage you to look on Pinterest for ideas and recipes. I use many different cutters and rollers and you don't have to buy expensive ones, using biscuit cutters and rolling pins from your cupboard is fine.[1]

---

1 For a great play dough recipe, see www.theimaginationtree.com/2012/04/ best-ever-no-cook-play-dough-recipe.html

I often talk to the children about how the dough feels and smells. Playing with play dough can be very open-ended, it allows children to be imaginative and creative and to experience and explore different textures and smells. If you are concerned about the mess ensure you have a mat on the table, and on the floor. Using play dough is usually one of the cleaner ways of doing sensory play. Play dough is also not just for younger children, I know many teens and primary school children who love play dough – if they see a pot they will often want to play, fiddle and explore with it.

Other sensory play ideas for the home

I often encourage parents to have a sensory play resource box, put away on a shelf or in a cupboard, that you can access and use when you are ready to do sensory play. There are always going to be times when the moment is not right for sensory play. You may be about to leave the house or have visitors, or about to cook tea. It is important as parents that we bring out sensory play when we are feeling ok about it; if you're feeling stressed and agitated sensory play with your children may just make those feelings worse!

Suggestions for things to go in your sensory play box

- bubbles – most children love bubbles. I usually carry a small pot of bubbles in my bag, there have been many an occasion in a meeting, church service, wedding, on a train and on a bus when I have whipped out my bubbles to calm or distract an agitated child

- play dough – bought or made
- pots of glitter – not just for Christmas!
- paper for drawing/painting/printing
- shredded paper – babies particularly love exploring shredded paper, filling a paddling pool with shredded paper is endless fun
- feathers – wonderful play with drawing on faces/on hands/ or sticking with
- dried pasta/rice/oats – have a container of this, children love running their hands through it, they love the feel and texture. You could dye the rice/pasta/oats different food colours. For an older child, you could thread the pasta. Have containers to fill and empty
- cotton wool balls – great texture, particularly good for children who aren't keen on the mess. Use them to paint with, rub them on skin, explore the gentleness of them
- baby lotion/hand cream – use for making hand/footprints, playing massage games, mark making
- paint and brushes – you can make your own paint, plenty of recipes on Pinterest for this
- chalks
- water – obviously you wouldn't have this in your box! But water is a wonderful form of sensory play, and if you are concerned about mess, think about bath time and bubbles and the play you can do at this time. Using ice cubes in play is really fun with very little mess. You can freeze small toys, flowers, treasures in the ice cubes
- crazy soap (this is soap in an aerosol can a bit like shaving foam) – great for mark making, add glitter, sequins to it, hide animals in it.

If the mess is something you find hard, the warmer weather is a great time to do sensory play outside, with less of an issue about containing the mess and an easy way to clean up the children afterwards by putting them in the paddling pool.

Important things to remember with sensory play and children include never leaving them on their own, only offering them things to play with that they can't choke on, if you have a child who puts everything in their mouth think very carefully about what you offer them.

Sensory play in the nursery and classroom

As practitioners we know that sensory play offers children many wonderful learning opportunities and many early years settings are excellent at offering children a wide variety of sensory play opportunities. Recently, through my nurture work, I have been reminded how easy it is as early years practitioners to think that children we see will have had some sensory opportunities. As I mentioned earlier increasingly I am finding this is not the case. Even the simplest opportunities may not have been available to all the children we work with. I have recently been playing a lot with bubbles through my nurture work; bubbles are a wonderful tool on many levels and bring so much joy to children, but I have sometimes found that even the experience of playing with bubbles can be new to some children.

Sensory play through nurture work – exploring emotions and feelings

In my role as a nurture worker I use sensory play every day; I mostly work with four-year-olds in reception classes. Using sensory play is a wonderful way to build up a trusting relationship with a child and can help to enhance their wellbeing. It is a fantastic way to help a child explore and develop their senses and to be in touch with their feelings and emotions. Often the sensory play activity I take into classes for the one child I am working with is then eagerly sought out by the rest of the children in the class.

Through using sensory play a child is able to safely explore different sensations and sensory play is a great vehicle for helping children understand their feelings. While using sensory play I will often talk to children about how it feels, for example, is it soft, hard, gooey, sticky? It is a great way to increase their vocabulary but also helps them to think about how it makes them feel. Do they like it? Does it make them feel scared? Does it make them laugh? Do they feel happy when they are playing with it? What feelings does it give inside their body? Does it make them feel warm inside or wobbly? Some sensory play can be really calming and soothing, I have observed children who are highly agitated and distressed really calm down when they are sitting down with a box of rice. Running their fingers through the rice helps them feel calmer, the sensation and the feel of the rice (or sand) brings about the same feelings, a sense of calmness and peacefulness.

Some children find sensory play very difficult, there are children who become really distressed at having dirty hands, sticky hands, etc. You are still able to do sensory play with these children by being sensitive to their concerns. You can make sensory bags/bottles with children, where you put sensory materials into a freezer bag or bottle and seal it. This allows children to play and explore but without the mess going all over them. You can then slowly introduce the child to more experiences that they can cope with, allowing the child to sit back and watch while you put your hands in the sensory material. Allow them to explore sensory materials at their pace, this may be tentatively dipping a finger in to start; by watching you enjoying it and exploring they will learn how it can be played with. One child I work with was very unsure about sensory play, over a few months, she slowly increased the amount of time she would tolerate being near the sensory play. Recently I took in crazy soap and by the end of the session she had her hands in the soap, she spread it on her arms and was laughing with delight.

Sensory play is inclusive

Sensory play is an excellent inclusive form of play. I have worked with many children with additional needs who are able to join in with the sensory activities with the rest of their class. Because sensory play is very free and non-directed, it is something that a child cannot fail at. For children who find play with others difficult (some children find it very hard to understand the 'rules' of play), sensory play can be a great way of helping children learn social skills, by playing alongside, having conversations about what they are playing with, how it feels, sharing it with others, watching how others are playing; this is a gentle and fun way of building children's social skills.

I have also found sensory play is a good way to help children with low self-esteem, because there is no right or wrong way to do sensory play. One boy I worked with didn't want to do any mark making, he would often say, 'I can't do it, I am no good at that.' I suggested that his key person started to use sand, rice, mud and sticks to do some mark making; slowly over the weeks of doing this, in a gentle fun way, with encouragement and through the key person showing him he was doing some writing, he began to believe in himself. Often early years settings and reception classes comment on how their boys are reluctant to mark make, starting them off with mark making in sensory play can often be an enticing and encouraging way forward for them.

Developing skills through sensory play

I firmly believe that sensory play needs to be part of our ongoing provision in the nursery or classroom. Many settings do this very well, although sometimes reception classes offer less sensory play. Sensory play is a fantastic way to help children develop the muscles in their hands, the skills they use through sensory play will help to develop the skills they will need for writing later on. Squeezing and rolling play dough, threading with pasta and buttons and ribbons, picking up cotton wool buds with tweezers, using pipettes to squirt warm water onto ice blocks, squeezing instant mashed potato through an icing bag, these are all excellent examples of children learning hand control, developing their muscles and helping them to manipulate objects. They are all vital skills that the children will need when they later learn to write. This is learning through play; these are just a few of the rich learning skills we need to offer to our children.

Heuristic play

The term heuristic play was first used by Elinor Goldschmied, it is a form of play which is open-ended, spontaneous and encourages exploration (Goldshmied and Jackson 1994). The dictionary definition of heuristic is enabling a hands-on and interactive approach to learning. Heuristic play is based on giving babies and young children natural and household objects to play with, allowing them to explore and discover in a safe way (Riddall-Leech 2009).

Heuristic play is open-ended and child led, it is based on the child exploring and discovering with all their senses. Heuristic play allows children to play with everyday objects, making them into whatever they want – there is no right or wrong way to do this type of play. The beauty of heuristic play is that you can use objects that you have in the home or natural objects that you have found.

Heuristic play encourages children to use their senses, exploring touch, sounds and taste, in a safe way. Often parents comment that a toddler's favourite game is to empty a drawer or cupboard. Early on in my career, one of the boys I nannied for loved emptying the kitchen cupboard, he would spend ages taking all the pots, pans and spoons out of the cupboard, he loved putting things in and out of each other. Looking back I can now see he showed signs of a containing schematic interest (Nutbrown 2011). If I had given him treasure baskets with household objects in this would have met his need and extended the interest he had in containing things, putting objects inside one another and would have saved the cupboards being emptied so often!

Treasure baskets are one aspect of heuristic play developed by Elinor Goldshmeid. These are containers which have a mix of natural or household objects in them. Treasure baskets were originally intended for babies who can sit up, but are not yet crawling or walking. The basket has different, safe objects that the baby can pull out and explore. The aim is to have objects in the basket which are made from natural materials, not plastic (Riddall-Leech 2009).

Examples of objects to put in a treasure basket

- wooden spoons
- loofah sponge/natural sponge
- different materials of different sizes, e.g. fleece/velvet/shimmery
- large shells
- large pebbles
- wooden nail brush/pastry brush
- scarves (wool, cotton, silk)
- small metal bowl
- corks
- egg cups
- a small bag of lavender seeds (sewn in the bag so cannot be emptied/eaten but can be smelt)
- wooden bangles
- metal bangles
- metal tea strainer

- metal spoons
- shredded paper.

Using treasure baskets

You need to ensure the items in your treasure basket are safe, and the baby can't choke on them. Remember, the baby will want to explore by putting things in their mouth. Allow the baby to explore and investigate, don't direct their play, but talk to them about what they are exploring, how it feels, sounds, tastes, etc., show them that you are interested in what they are playing by being alongside them, smiling and gently encouraging them and being curious about them. Make sure babies are not left alone with the treasure basket.

Heuristic play with toddlers and older children

Heuristic play with older children is again about offering children everyday and natural objects for children to play and explore with. These are objects which are not obvious toys, they are not plastic items that have only one purpose.

I have used heuristic play with children and teenagers. Often parents comment that young children prefer the cardboard box instead of the toy inside. The cardboard box offers them a wealth of opportunities – it can be so many different things from a spacecraft to a castle to an elephant, a robot or a den.

Heuristic play offers children so much potential for imaginative learning and opportunities. For several years, I co-created and ran a play venue called Messy Space at a Christian arts festival called Greenbelt. Messy Space was a play venue for all ages; it had a mix of toys, creative opportunities and most importantly a large amount of heuristic play. It was wonderful to see the wide range of children (including teenagers) that played with these items. Some children used the opportunity to make things – rockets, boats and dens – others used it to explore, wrap, hide things. Many parents commented on the simplicity of the materials and play resources and were amazed at how much fun children had and how much time children spent with them. We often think of using these things with younger children but forget that older children also gain much from being allowed heuristic play.

Examples of heuristic play materials for older children

- cardboard boxes
- tubes of different sizes
- string
- wool
- masking tape
- material of different sizes and textures
- rope
- netting
- buttons
- corks
- sponge
- bubble wrap
- containers of different sizes and shapes
- cotton reels

- pine cones, conkers, acorns
- pebbles, shells
- feathers
- sticks.

How you offer heuristic play to children

When you offer children heuristic play think carefully about what you are offering them and how you offer it. Sometimes I see a junk modelling corner in a nursery, which has a few squashed boxes and children are expected to create something, this rarely looks enticing. If offering heuristic play is a new thing for your setting/home, spend some time thinking about what and how you are offering it. We need to offer children resources in a way which gives them value and worth. Lay out the material in a way which looks interesting and sparks some curiosity. Make sure what you are offering is safe, looks interesting, encourage the children to explore and see what you have laid out for them. Importantly, explain to the children, for whom this may be new, that they are materials they can play with and create whatever they want. Some children will want to make something, others will be happy improvising the materials into new play items and will find other things to enhance the play. This is about child-led play, be alongside them, observe and gently encourage and show curiosity.

Sensory play, heuristic play and wellbeing

I believe heuristic and sensory play is brilliant for children of all ages; the open-ended nature of the play, the opportunity to explore, discover and experiment are all things which are essential to help children feel good about who they are and help them to discover more about what they like, dislike and what they can do; it helps to enhance their wellbeing. Because there is no right or wrong way to play with sensory play and heuristic play, it helps a child to grow in confidence and can be an opportunity for a child to try out new things. Heuristic play and sensory play are also excellent because they cost very little, if any, money. You are able to use many recycled materials and things you have in your home or work. Locally, we have a scrap store which is full of recycled materials from local businesses, for a small membership fee a year and a small contribution you are able to get a rich range of heuristic play materials. Scrap stores are worth being members of.

Sensory play for children who cannot sit still

In schools now and sometimes in nursery, we expect children to sit on the carpet or at a desk for extended periods of time. I have real concerns about how realistic our expectations are in terms of how long we are expecting children to sit and I think we often have the balance wrong, but there are times when it is necessary. Some children find this very hard, they wriggle, they fidget, they move, they poke other children, they lie down and roll around or they just get up and walk away. During the last two years, I have been discovering sensory fiddle toys that can help with this. Traditionally these have been offered to children with attention deficit hyperactivity disorder (ADHD) or autism spectrum disorder (ASD). I have also found them to be useful for lots of other children, for example children who are anxious, children who are feeling excited, children who are finding it hard to concentrate. I have also found they work really well across the ages, from young children as a distraction to primary children and teenagers who are anxious or have ADHD or dyspraxia and find it hard to concentrate.

Examples of fiddle toys suitable for children aged 3+

- tangles – toys you can hold in your hand and continuously move[2]
- stress balls
- small stretch toys, e.g. men, lizards, frogs (only use with children who don't put things in their mouth)
- beanie toys which are soft to touch – soft bean bag inside soft toy.

Sensory play to calm children

Some children become very anxious and distressed. Sensory play can really help with this. Offering children very calming sensory play can be a way to help bring down their heightened senses. I have often used homemade lavender

---

2   www.tinknstink.co.uk/shop-by-brand/tangle-creations.html

play dough, massage games, rice play, and made calming bottles. Calming bottles are small plastic water bottles with water, glitter, and glycerin added, they work like snow globes. I have also added shells, loom bands or water beads into these bottles. Secure the top onto the bottle with glue and get the child to shake it, then watch as it all settles. These work really well as a calming aid.

Questions for practice and reflection

■ Are you using sensory play and heuristic play regularly in your setting or home?

■ Have you got a range of resources that you can use in sensory play?

■ Do you use sensory play to help calm children as well at times of exploring and investigating?

■ Do you explain to parents the benefits of sensory play and offer ideas and suggestions of how they can do this at home?

References

Beckerleg, T. (2009) *Fun with Messy Play*. London: Jessica Kingsley Publishers.

Gainsley, S. (2011) 'Look, listen, touch, feel, taste: The importance of sensory play.' Available at www.highscope.org/file/NewsandInformation/Extensions/ExtVol25No5_low.pdf, accessed on 31/01/16.

Gascoyne, S. (2013) *Sensory Play – Play in the EYFS*. London: Practical Pre-School Books.

Goldschmied, E. and Jackson, S. (1994) *People Under Three: Young Children in Day Care* (2nd edition). Abingdon: Routledge.

Nutbrown, C. (2011) *Threads of Thinking* (4th edition). London: Sage.

Riddall-Leech, S. (2009) *Heuristic Play – Play in the EYFS.* London: Practical Pre-School Books.

Sunderland, M. (2006) *What Every Parent Needs to Know.* London: Dorling Kindersley Limited.

Chapter 5

Creativity

The term creativity can be quite scary for some adults. If you had a negative experience in school with creative subjects, as an adult you may still carry a feeling of dread and panic at the idea of doing something 'creative'. This was my experience for a long time – I find drawing and painting very hard, I dislike singing, I can't play a musical instrument and I feel deeply awkward at the idea of acting! The creative subjects at school left me feeling inadequate and a failure. Fortunately, I met and then married an artist! He helped me to see that creativity is so much more than being able to draw or dance. Creativity is more than just the 'arts'. Creativity is as much about how you view the world, how you engage with life, how you have creative ideas and problem solve as well as how you make things.

Ken Robinson (2015) proposes that creativity is about using your imagination; he argues that everyone has the potential to be creative and that creativity is part of all areas of life, for example engineering, technology, art, teaching, mathematics and sciences.

A child's right to creativity

Under Article 31 of the United Nations Convention on the Rights of the Child (UNICEF n.d.), it states that all children have a right to play, relax and have artistic activities. We often hear this article quoted in relation to a child's right to play, but don't hear so often about the right to artistic activities.

Creativity in the early years

Within the early years foundation stage (DFES 2007), the importance of having an emphasis on creativity and the arts is recognised through having a specific area of learning and development with the focus on 'Expressive arts and Design' (DFES 2007). This recognises the need for children to be encouraged and enabled to explore, investigate, experiment and be curious.

An organisation called Earlyarts[1] encourages people to think about creativity and playfulness as being linked. I often hear early years workers comment that they are not creative as they unable to make a beautiful finished product, but they are playful; they often see play as being a process and 'art' as being creative. Both creativity and playfulness are important and are linked; by encouraging creativity and imagination both through play and through experiencing, we are helping children to develop and strengthen the neural pathways in their brains (Churchill-Dower 2014).

To enable and allow children to be creative, I believe we need to be open to being creative ourselves. We need to be willing to explore our own creativity, this might be through

---

1   www.earlyarts.co.uk

drawing, sculpting, writing, dancing, acting, singing, comedy, but also other ways we often don't think of, for example I believe cooking can be a really creative act. My eldest daughter is a great cook but gets deeply bored by following recipes; she has the confidence to be creative and experiment, sometimes these experiments are less edible but most of the time they are great. Gardening can also be very creative.

Questions for practice and reflection

- How do you view creativity, is this something you are open to and actively encourage or something you feel awkward about?
- What do you do for yourself that is creative and allows that part of your being to flourish?
- Do you value creativity as much as other types of learning? How do you show this in your practice?

Supporting and valuing children's creativity

So often, as adults, we can be gate keepers to children, particularly younger children. If our experience of creativity is negative, if we feel that we can't do it or feel awkward, then this is often picked up by the children. If we don't really value creativity then this message is also passed on to children. Sadly I have seen many children bring home amazing creations from nursery or school, hand them over to their parents as they are collected and the parent barely looks at the creation or worse still makes a negative comment and throws it away in the nearby bin. I have observed this time and time again and watched children's faces look so sad and hurt. As early years professionals, we have as much of a duty to explain to parents the importance of creativity as we do to emphasise to parents the importance of reading to their child.

The other challenge with allowing children to be creative is the adults who need to be in control. I have seen so often adults who are quick to tell children where to stick things, how something should look, instead of allowing children to try it out, create and discover for themselves. Sometimes this comes from adults' need to be in control but I also wonder if at other times it is about adults not allowing themselves to develop their own creativity and instead trying to express this through the children. Curiously, I have noticed this particularly in some senior school art teachers! The best art teachers I know are those who are also developing their own artwork outside work. Artists and creative people often say that an essential element to being creative is the letting go, allowing an idea to have the time to develop; you often hear of writers who describe how, when they start writing their book, they don't really know how the story will develop.

How we introduce creativity to young children

Introducing children to creativity can start from within the womb. We know that talking to and singing to the unborn baby helps to develop their brain and the parents' attachment with the unborn baby. In the last trimester, the sound processing parts of the brain are working and the unborn baby is able to hear voices and sound patterns

(Skwarecki 2013). They become familiar with the unique rhythm and tones of the mother's voice.[2] This is why a newborn baby will turn towards the voice of its mother and other familiar voices, such as the father or siblings.

Newborn babies love being sung to and talked to. It is wonderful to see the great joy a young baby gets from 'talking' with their caregiver. The interaction, the talking to, looking at, waiting for the baby to talk back are all wonderful ways of building the baby's wellbeing and strengthening the attachment. With singing, it doesn't matter how good your singing is, babies often adore it! I said earlier in the chapter I am not keen on singing, but I am more than happy to sing with young children. When my girls were tiny babies I often used to sing the first verse of 'You are my sunshine' (Davis 1939) to them. I still remember fondly the way this would calm them, how they would gaze at me and smile. Neuroscientists have now found that the brain has specific and specialised areas that respond only to music and that these areas stimulate emotional responses (Sousa 2006).

As babies grow into toddlers they often continue to love singing and dancing. How many YouTube videos or Facebook clips have you seen of toddlers joyfully dancing? My husband and I both worked part time and shared caring for our children when they were little. My husband would often spend time on his days with the girls dancing around the kitchen, or playing his guitar for them to dance to. This brought all of them so much joy and great laughter. Margot Sunderland (2006) uses the phrase 'joy juice', which I love. She uses this to describe those moments of intense joyfulness,

---

2   www.zerotothree.org

feeling alive and wonderfully happy. The moments when our brains release dopamine and opioids, chemicals which enhance our feelings of wellbeing.

Neuroscientists have found that children with more music skills often have a greater development in reading skills later in life (Kay 2016). They have also found the area of the brain that is used for developing music skills is also used for developing mathematical skills. It is believed that encouraging and enabling young children to experience singing and experimenting with sounds, rhythms, noises and musical instruments helps to strengthen the young child's brain, which in turn will help their further learning and development. As my children grew older I would often play them different types of music – fast, slow, melancholy, exciting. I would talk to them about how it made them feel, if they liked it, if it made them feel sad or happy. This was an excellent way of linking creativity with feelings and emotions.

The first years of a child's life are vital for their brain development; by offering children creative, cultural and imaginative experiences we are helping our young children's brains to develop, this will enable them to go on and explore, learn, discover new things as they grow.[3]

Questions for practice and reflection

- How much singing do you do with your child/children?
- Do you play different types of music to your children?

---

3   www.earlyarts.co.uk

■ How much opportunity is there to dance? If you feel uncomfortable about doing this yourself you could find some pre-school dance programmes on the TV or YouTube to watch with the children.

Having space and time to be creative

An essential element in helping children to be creative is giving them space to develop their own ideas; as adults, we need to know when to stand back and watch how they are developing and carefully decide when to step in and assist them (Craft, McConnon and Paige-Smith 2012). When children have time and space they develop ideas, try out new things, problem solve. These are all using creative skills, which help children's development and learning.

Part of being creative is having the space to think and ask questions. Craft (2007) describes this as 'possibility thinking'. It's the moments when children have the space to look at something and think 'What if...' It's the confidence to ask the 'what if' questions and then the confidence to try something new and explore an idea, this then leads to children's extended thinking and learning.

Creativity needs time; children need to have time to develop their ideas, try something out. Often children find it very distressing if they are being rushed to finish something, for example the picture they are making or the den they are building.

Creativity in Reggio Emilia

Reggio Emilia is a town in northern Italy where, since the 1940s, they have been developing a unique way of educating pre-school children. This was originally started by a group of mothers who were unhappy with the education system, and was developed by educationist Loris Malaguzzi; the town developed their own 'Reggio approach' to education. This approach embeds creativity and the recognition that children express themselves through 'a hundred different languages' (Edwards, Gandini and Forman 1998). The Reggio approach stems from the belief that every child is a unique, strong and competent learner. As educators, they see their role as listening to and understanding how each individual child is communicating and they also see the role of an educator as being a co-learner alongside each child. Each Reggio pre-school has a full-time artist and an art room as part of their setting. The artist works closely with the educators and the children together; the artists and the educators think very carefully about the materials they offer to the children and give careful thought to how the children may respond to the material. They encourage children from a very young age to really look and notice, to be curious and see detail and also to explore materials; their focus is about children engaging with and exploring textures and materials.

I was really fortunate to go on a study tour to Reggio Emilia and to attend a children's rights conference. As part of this tour, I visited several early years settings. I was particularly struck by how each setting beautifully and artistically presented the children's work. The work is often about the process and has less emphasis on the finished perfect piece. It is also about children's imaginative and creative work rather than children copying other 'artists' work, as I see so often in the UK. Each piece is presented as it would be in a gallery, with value and beauty. The attention to detail in the environment, making it a beautiful, rich and stimulating place, is an important part of the Reggio approach.

One particular aspect of the Reggio pedagogy is the encouragement of following children's interests and the documentation of children's learning. The Reggio Emilia nurseries have become well known not just for their creative way of working with children but also for the way they carefully document the children's learning. They now have a large and rich archive of material going back to when they started documenting children's work in the 1940s.

One of the unique ways they work with children in Reggio is through the recognition they give to the time and space needed to develop creative ideas. Their work is based on children's interests and ideas and helping to develop these. When I was in Reggio I saw an example of one pre-school that had been working on a project about shoes. This started out with children walking down a narrow street in the city and noticing all the shoe shops (of which there are many!). The children noticed the different shapes, sizes and colours. The children wanted to talk about the shoes and tell their friends about the shoes. The staff encouraged the children to draw the shoes, to talk about the shoes, to think about the details they saw on the shoes, to think about the stories behind the shoes – what they are used for, who wore them, etc. Over the weeks and months, the children drew pictures of shoes, made models of shoes, designed shoes and then made clay models of shoes. These shoes were then displayed on a special art day where all the children in the pre-schools display their artwork to the city. These shoes were displayed outside the shoe shop for the day and were admired by many. The staff and the children also made a book about their shoes.

This project was a beautiful exploration of children's interest and imagination. It was a lovely example of how, when given the time, space and support, children can create some beautiful pieces of artwork. There are many things that I found inspiring about the Reggio model, but what stood out was the space children are given to explore their own interests, with staff working alongside the children, listening to their ideas but also actively co-exploring and co-working with the children. This relationship is a careful balance – sometimes the child leads, sometimes the adult offers ideas – this requires an active engagement and trust on both sides. The adults recognise their roles as being co-explorers. I was also impressed by the community's response to the children's work and the way the whole community encouraged the children's creativity. I cannot imagine a town in the UK yearly having a day where all the early years settings in the town display their artwork, and most people from the city come to see it and celebrate the children's work.

Reggio-inspired work outside of Italy

There is an organisation called Sightlines in the UK which supports creativity and reflective practice and links settings in the UK to Reggio pre-schools.[4] There are also groups across the country which support the creative practice of early years settings and are inspired by the work in Reggio. There is a Facebook Reggio group and Reggio pins on Pinterest. In the city where I live, Bath, there is a group called 5x5x5 which brings together early years settings, artists, mentors and cultural settings to work creatively with the children.[5] For several years I worked as a mentor on this project. I had an inspiring time working with several different early years settings, schools and artists on projects which promoted children's creativity, followed their interests, co-explored with the children and documented the learning. Following on from this project I have supported several nurseries in the UK to think about how they can use the Reggio principles in their daily work. (I share a story from one of those nurseries in Chapter 6.) The challenge for settings outside of Reggio is to think about how to embed this practice in an authentic way for your setting. We can't take a carbon copy of what is happening in the early years settings in Reggio, but there are practices and ideas that we can draw on, reflect on and embed in our practice. There are various blogs where people discuss their experience of how they develop ideas from Reggio or Malaguzzi in their setting. One blogger from Sweden develops and shares some really useful questions and ideas from her practice (Axelsson 2016).

---

4   www.sightlines-initiative.com./our-work.html
5   https://5x5x5creativity.org.uk

Thinking about the resources we offer to children

If we want children to have creative opportunities, if we value their time and creative processes, then we need to think very carefully about what resources we offer them. So many times I have been in early years settings which offer an 'arts' corner or a 'craft' corner, and it consists of a box of waxed crayons which look like they have been rolled on the floor for the last five years, some felt-tip pens with lids missing, a few scrappy bits of paper and maybe some dried out glue. I know this sounds like an extremely bleak view, but, unfortunately, I have seen this many many times. If we want to value creativity then we need to show this through the materials we present and the way we present them. We don't have to spend lots of money, but we do need to ensure that the resources are well stocked and looked after. I have seen some great examples of creative areas, which look inviting, exciting and encourage children to be curious and creative. In the Reggio settings, they have a selection of small parts/small resources for children to access, these are presented in a beautiful way, they look inviting, interesting and create curiosity. I am a firm believer in teaching and explaining to children how to look after the arts area; we need to explain that this is an area where they can create and experiment but that it needs looking after, and show them how they should look after it.

Examples of what could be in your creative corner

This is not an exhaustive list but one to start you off:

- wax crayons (which are not old and fluffy!)
- crayons
- pens (with lids on)
- pastels
- chalks
- pots of different types of material, e.g. velvet, leather, lace, cord, denim
- pots of small pieces of different coloured paper and types of paper, e.g. card, shiny
- pots with things to stick, e.g. tin foil, plastic bottle tops, pieces of wool, corks, beads, shells, buttons
- small boxes, toilet roll holders, yoghurt pots, small tubs
- glue

- cellophane – great for providing colour and looking through
- sellotape
- double sided tape
- masking tape
- string
- glitter
- pieces of paper and card of different sizes
- buttons
- wooden lollipop sticks
- wooden pegs.

It's about the process and the experience, not the end product

So often creativity is seen to be about the end product, particularly with drawing, painting and modelling; however, children need to be able to have the chance to experiment, investigate and be creative without necessarily creating an end product. The process children go through in mixing paint, layering things on top of each other, wrapping something, these are all important learning opportunities with the child investigating and being curious. So often we ask children, 'What have you made?' and they don't always know, it often isn't meant to be something, but was more about the doing. The doing is great, instead of asking what something is you could say to the child, 'Tell me about this, how did you make it?' By showing curiosity and interest you are encouraging the child and helping them to feel good about this process.

Introducing young children to using art materials

We are able to offer babies the opportunity to experience creative materials. You need to think carefully because they may try to eat everything they are offered, but you can make paint with yoghurt and food colouring and also offer different food types that they can experiment with. Sargent (2016) describes an art project with babies where they used a large piece of paper for babies and toddler to sit on and they offered spinach, raspberries and spices for the children to explore with their hands, feet and bodies. This very tactile experience is a great way for young children to have the experience of early mark making.

Move away from templates

When I started out in my career I worked as a student in a reception class. Early on in the term the children were asked to draw a picture of a tree, an example that the teacher had made earlier was shown to the children. One child in the class painted his tree purple; he spent ages on this tree, he spent a long time thinking about the colour and painting the different leaves. The TA in the class looked at his picture and told him off because his tree was not green like everyone else's and like the picture he was shown. He was asked, 'When do you ever see purple trees?' This memory has stayed with me. At the time I remember thinking, 'Why can't his tree be purple?' This was over 25 years ago, but I still see settings use templates and pictures they made earlier for the children to copy. Asking children to copy pictures is not about creativity, it is about adults being controlling. As a parent, I did not want my child bringing home a picture that looked identical to everyone else's, that they could not be sure if it was theirs if it hadn't their name on it.

Often I am told by staff that they have to do this style of creativity, particularly for Mother's Day or Christmas, because parents expect it. I would suggest that it is helpful to explain to parents the value of children creating and making their own pictures. I know one setting that informs parents as part of their policy that they value children's creativity and they will not be sending out 'perfect' Christmas and Mother's Day cards made by the children. Duffy (2006) suggests that mass-produced artwork is not creative and does not encourage creative ideas or creative thinking. I think it is fine to give children an idea, showing them an example, but we need to ensure we are not forcing children to all make identikits of the picture. We need to encourage children to be inspired by things they see but not force them into copying what they see. We want to encourage children to have their own ideas, to experiment. I believe the emphasis needs to be on their work and their ideas and we want them to feel good about what they have made.

Being inspired by artists, not recreating their pictures

The other use of the template model you often see is children being asked to recreate pictures by famous artists, this seems particularly popular in reception classes. So many times I have visited schools where they have artwork in the corridors copying Monet's Waterlilies or

Van Gogh's Sunflowers. There is something amazing about seeing the real Sunflowers paintings and the real Waterlilies, I personally have been brought to tears standing in front of these paintings in Paris and Amsterdam, and I love to show young children artwork and see how they respond to it. But this is different to showing children a badly copied image of the Sunflowers and asking children to copy it. It is good to use artists' work to show as an example to children, but this should be used as a starting point not as an end point. The skill is in helping children to explore the picture and talk about how it makes them feel, to consider which colours have been used and why. Use this as a starting point for them to explore and be creative not an end point to making a picture the same.

Questions for practice and reflection

- Do you have a member of staff who is responsible for your art area? Do they daily restock and check it?
- How does your art area look? Does it look loved and valued or is it a bit of a mess in the corner? Could you bring it back to life?
- How do you display children's work? Do you give value to what they make by displaying work regularly and carefully?
- Do your staff feel able to allow children to create and make, or do they feel the urge to correct them? Maybe staff need support in exploring this idea.
- Do you tell parents about the importance of allowing children to create and explore and that as a setting you value their creativity, which means you won't send out 'perfect' Mother's Day cards?

Storytelling

Children use storytelling and imagination and pretending often in their play. Children from as young as one year old start to use pretending in their play and by the ages of three and four this is really well embedded into many children's play (Gopnik 2016). I remember watching and listening to my daughters when they were young, speaking out, telling the story in their play with pirates, playmobil figures and farm animals. I was often amazed at their language and the complexity of their stories. Telling stories, playing stories, acting out stories are wonderful examples of how creative young children can be. But is storytelling something we encourage? As educators do we actively listen out for the many stories children are telling? Do we recognise the deep learning taking place during this storytelling? I have been really inspired by Vivian Gussin-Paley (1990), she wrote a book focusing on storytelling in the classroom. As a teacher she realised that she was not giving time and space to the children's stories, she was not recognising the important role they had in the life of the class. She found that she used to dismiss the stories and not recognise the essential element of children sharing in each other's stories. At one stage she used to stop children interrupting to ask questions about the other children's stories, but as time went on, she realised that the questioning and commenting on each other's stories were essential to learning and to the development of the story; they were an essential part of a shared process, a shared language. Children often use storytelling to work out issues or try out ideas; storytelling can be a safe way for children to explore new ideas and thoughts. Vivian Gussin-Paley encouraged the children she worked with to tell stories and act out their stories.

Questions for practice and reflection

- How do you listen to and document the stories children tell?
- How do you encourage children's storytelling? Are you inquisitive and curious with them about their stories?
- How do you encourage the children to share their stories and act out their stories?
- How much attention do you give to children's storytelling? Do you give it the same amount of attention as music or drawing?

What do young children need to encourage their creativity?

We know that children are born with curiosity, interest and fascination, they are born with creativity (Duffy 2006). It is the role of parents and educators to nurture and encourage this, and enable children to develop. Children learn through doing, trying, creating and exploring. It is vital that we enable this and help children to develop these skills. We need to give children time, space and encouragement to explore the world with all their senses; through developing this, they are being allowed to develop their creative responses and interests.

Offering children a wide variety of opportunities helps to make the connections in their brain stronger (Churchill-Dower 2014).

A wide and rich range of opportunities

We need to offer our children a wide and rich range of creative opportunities. Some of this is about the continuous provision we offer, for example, dressing up clothes for imaginative storytelling and play, art resources, musical instruments, the opportunity for laughter and telling jokes. There are many other creative opportunities we can introduce, such as visiting an art gallery, seeing large paintings and sculptures, taking children to gardens and museums, exploring the colours, scents and sights in a garden. We can teach children to cook, tasting different foods and exploring different smells and textures of food. We can reading poetry to children, young children love rhyming words and phrases. Watching a play or a dance can inspire creativity in children and doesn't have to mean a trip to the theatre – CBeebies have recently done a *Midsummer Night's Dream* for young children, which can be found online. Recently I visited a photographic exhibition of creatures in the sea, I observed a toddler of around two years old looking at each photo with his dad; it was wonderful to see the way the dad interacted with the little boy, talking to him about each of the photos; the boy was totally engaged and fascinated by what he was seeing, he was animated and responded with a look of awe, excitement and many comments.

How creativity, creative learning and wellbeing are connected

An important element of creativity and creative learning is having the space to find out and experiment. We know that children learn through the hands-on doing and repeating. If we see using all our senses as an important part of creativity, then we can see how young children particularly learn in this way. Sensory play is wonderfully creative, enabling children to learn, develop and discover in an open-ended way. I discussed this in more detail in Chapter 4.

Questions for practice and reflection

- How much time and consideration do you and your staff give to creativity?
- What are the different creative resources and opportunities that you offer to children? Could you expand these?
- How do you and your staff show that you value the learning taking place through creative practice? Does this get as much attention as the learning taking place through other forms of opportunities and play?
- Do you have opportunities for your children to explore a wide range of creative activities? Have you visited a museum, garden or art gallery with the children? Have you had dancers perform for your children, could you link up with a local dance school?
- Do your staff team need some professional development looking at creativity?

References

Axelsson, S. (2016) Interaction Imagination (blog). Available at www.interactionimagination.blogspot.co.uk, accessed on 29/08/16.

Churchill-Dower, R. (2014) *Teddy Talks: Bonkers about Brains: Creativity and Brain Development in Children.* Available at www.youtube.com/watch?v=ssvWfelKxEI, accessed on 29/04/16.

Craft, A. (2007) 'Creativity and possibility in the early years.' Available at www.tactyc.org.uk/pdfs/Reflection-craft.pdf, accessed on 10/05/16.

Craft, A., McConnon, L. and Paige-Smith, A. (2012) 'Child-initiated play and professional creativity: Enabling four-year-olds' possibility thinking.' Available at http://oro.open.ac.uk/31395/2/Child_initiated_play.pdf, accessed on 30/12/15.

Davis, J. (1939) 'You are my sunshine.' Lyrics available at www.metrolyrics.com/you-are-my-sunshine-lyrics-willie-nelson.html, accessed on 29/04/16.

DFES (2007) Development Matters in the Early Years Foundation Stage (EYFS). Available at www.foundationyears.org.uk/files/2012/03/Development-Matters-FINAL-PRINT-AMENDED.pdf, accessed on 15/12/16.

Duffy, B. (2006) *Supporting Creativity and Imagination in the Early Years.* Milton Keynes: Open University Press.

Edwards, C., Gandini, L. and Forman, G. (1998) *The Hundred Languages of Children: The Reggio Emilia Approach – Advanced Reflections.* London: Alex Publishing.

Gopnik, A. (2016) *The Gardener and the Carpenter: What the new science of child development tells us about the relationship between parents and children.* London: Penguin.

Gussin-Paley, V. (1990) *The Boy who Would Be a Helicopter: The Uses of Storytelling in the Classroom.* Harvard, MA: Harvard University Press.

Kay, M. (2016) 'Literacy through music.' Available at http://tactyc.org.uk/wp-content/uploads/2016/03/Maria-Kay-Reflections-article.docx, accessed on 30/10/16.

Robinson, K. (2015) 'Creativity is in everything, especially teaching.' Available at http://ww2.kqed.org/mindshift/2015/04/22/sir-ken-robinson-creativity-is-in-everything-especially-teaching, accessed on 29/04/16.

Sargent, M. (2016) 'Edible art.' *Nursery World,* 8–21 August.

Skwarecki, B. (2013) 'Babies learn to recognize words in the womb.' Available at www.sciencemag.org/news/2013/08/babies-learn-recognize-words-womb, accessed on 29/04/16.

Sousa, D. (2006) 'How arts develop the young brain.' Available at www.aasa.org/SchoolAdministratorArticle.aspx?id=7378, accessed on 29/04/16.

Sunderland, M. (2006) *What Every Parent Needs to Know.* London: Dorling Kindersley Limited.

UNICEF Fact Sheet (n.d.) 'A summary of the rights under the Convention on the Rights of the Child.' Available at www.unicef.org/crc/files/Rights_overview.pdf, accessed on 19/12/15.

Chapter 6

Exploring and Co-adventuring Together

Children love to learn, they are born inquisitive and curious, they want to find out and discover. As adults, we need to enable and offer children opportunities to develop this learning.

I love the way children are eager to share their passion and current interest with you, the way children soak up information, their enthusiasm and excitement to tell you about what they have found out. Over the last year, in my nurture work, I have learnt lots about sharks, what they eat, how they swim, where they live. I have also learnt quite a bit about superheroes, especially Spider-man – what he can do, what he can't do, who his friends are. The children who have told me these facts find learning in school quite hard, but when you link in to their passion and their interest, they begin to fly with their learning. If we really listen to children, if we hear what excites them and, if we include that in our planning, then children are more likely to engage with the learning and tasks they are being set. The child who adored superheroes was in a reception class and was refusing to engage with any maths and number work, he was convinced he could not do it. When his TA started to use superheroes in the maths, he was drawn in, he would happily count how many Spider-men were on a page or work out if there were less Superman than Spider-man pictures. This was a simple adaption, but one that helped this boy to feel that he could learn; he soon realised that he could count and grew in confidence.

Children's interests and wellbeing

We know that babies are born with billions of brain cells and that these need to be activated and stimulated to connect and make synapses; this activation enables the brain to develop. When children are interested, curious and deeply involved and engaged in an activity their brain is making new connections (Ephgrave 2015). As adults we need to discover what fascinates and excites children, what do they become deeply engaged in and fascinated by? We also need to ask the question about how can we support them in exploring these interests.

Wellbeing and involvement scale

Ferre Laevers (2015) has developed a wellbeing and involvement scale which many early years settings use. This includes a five-point scale measuring how engaged a child is in an activity. Laevers argues that children first need to feel confident in being able to explore and try things out, knowing that their needs are met. This is a sign of them having a good wellbeing; he then argues that children need to have good levels of involvement. This requires a carefully planned and enriching environment. Laevers proposes that a high level of involvement requires complete concentration and absorption in an activity. The Laevers wellbeing and involvement scale helps adults to identify and measure a child's involvement.

Think about a child who is totally engaged in an activity, think about how they look; often they have a look of total concentration, sometimes they will be sticking their tongue out, they are often not aware of what is going on around them, they are totally in that moment. Laevers argues at these moments of total involvement, children are learning a huge amount. Along with the wellbeing and involvement scale, Laevers has also developed ten action points to help adults increase children's wellbeing and involvement. These include providing a space that looks appealing and attractive, observing the children to find out what their interests are and then providing materials and resources that fit with these interests.

Questions for practice and reflection

- How often do you observe your children in times of complete engagement and involvement?
- What is it that completely captivates your children? If you are a key person think about your key children, can you name

what completely engages them and excites them? If you are a parent what is it that your child can engage in for an extended period of time?

If you're not sure of the answer to the above question, spend some time watching and observing, looking out for the moments of complete involvement. The Laevers scale can help you with this.

Moving away from rigid plans

When I first trained as an NNEB (National Nursery Examining Board – an old childcare diploma) over 25 years ago, you could often predict what topics and activities would be covered in nurseries and pre-schools across the country depending on the time of year. Autumn always brought in leaf painting, Christmas obviously brought in the Christmas trees and Santa pictures, Spring always brought in the life cycle of a frog, with fiddly pictures and diagrams to cut out and Summer always covered summer holidays. Now, in theory, there is nothing wrong with this, I know many children who love watching frog spawn turn to tadpoles and then into frogs, I still find that exciting, and of course it is great to cover Christmas. My irritation with this is that it can become a very lazy and uncreative way of working and, importantly, it doesn't take account of children's current interests. I often observed there was little new imagination or creativity that went into the ideas and the planning, this meant that often staff were bored and uninspired, which in turn affected the children.

One of my roles, when I worked for a children's charity, was to support early years settings in how they listen to children; part of this role was to visit, support, encourage and train early years settings. I started this job in around 2000, and I was still seeing quite a lot of settings using the same templates and planning that I had seen when I had first trained. For this reason, I was very supportive of the early years foundation stage (EYFS) guidance on planning which set out that plans should be flexible enough to adapt to children's interests (DCSF 2008). We went through a time when many settings embraced this and became more flexible in their plans. However, over the last couple of years, I have seen some settings return to the old style of planning. I think this has come about through settings feeling under increasing pressure and so using medium and long term plans, which they have used previously. They feel under increased pressure with workload and it makes life a bit easier. I really do understand the pressure that staff experience, but I would like to suggest that, by following children's interests, being responsive and adaptive in your planning, you will enhance the children's wellbeing and it can also help the staff to feel excited, motivated and more engaged in their work.

Car engines and small children

I have worked with one nursery for several years; all their planning is based on children's interests. I went in to see them once and several children had been talking about cars and were excited about cars. The room leader was married to a mechanic. The day I arrived they had a car engine in the room, in a tough spot, along with various tools, such as wrenches, pliers and sockets, and copies of Haynes car manuals. When I arrived a group of children were sitting at the engine, taking

Promoting Young Children's Emotional Health and Wellbeing

it apart, using the tools, talking about what they were doing. As I sat and talked to the children one little boy held up a small part from the car, he asked me if I knew what it was and I told him that I didn't. His reply was, 'It's a spark plug if the car ain't got one it can't go.' As I sat and observed the children, I could see the enthusiasm and interest from all the children in the room, they were all engaged with the car engine in different ways. Some were sitting with the engine and exploring it, others were looking at the manuals, others were drawing cars and some were using the tools with other items in the room. This was a room full of engaged, motivated, interested children who were learning in a creative way. The extension to the children's language development was also noticeable – the questions they were asking, the words they were using. Staff were alongside the children learning with the children and scaffolding the children's learning. After working in this way for a few months the staff commented on how much the children's language had developed in ways the staff had not expected.

What I love about this example is the creative thinking of staff, the ability of staff to think outside the box. I don't know many people who would plan ahead for a car engine in the nursery. It worked at that time because the children were interested. The staff told me they were really enjoying the creativity it allowed them as staff. By really listening to the children and tuning into what excites them, the staff are able to plan to meet the children's needs, meet the requirement of the EYFS and to be creative while doing this.

The influence of Reggio Emilia practice

For the nursery mentioned above, they had been really influenced by the work in Reggio Emilia, as discussed in Chapter 5. One challenge in this country is how to learn from the practice in Reggio and then how to develop it into something which is authentic and fits with the setting here in the UK, another challenge is how to embed this way, this ethos. So often, I see settings taking in some ideas, for example, forest school or Reggio practice; they try it out for a bit and then it fizzles out. I believe the challenge is in how you embed something new and this takes time, staff training and commitment from managers and staff. An essential underpinning ethos and belief in the Reggio practice is that children have rights now, that children have ideas, interests and will express themselves in one hundred different ways (Edwards, Gandini and Forman 1998). As adults, we need to tune in, listen, support and give the children space to explore and learn.

Allowing children space to explore

Settings that choose to follow children's interests and use this fully in their planning can find that the learning from the children can exceed what the adults initially thought they were capable of. When we use children's interests and fascination, when we use these moments and interests to help teach and scaffold their learning, we find that children make progress and extend their knowledge and interests. By adults coming alongside them, engaging with them, sharing their curiosity and interest, co-learning and co-exploring with them, children are able to develop and extend their knowledge and skills. Anna Ephgrave (2015) describes in her book how all the planning in the nursery and reception classes is based on 'in the moment' retrospective planning; they write up the children's learning, the interaction and the outcome afterwards, they do not plan ahead of time. This is similar practice to the nursery I mentioned in the car engine example. Ephgrave (2015) argues that having a very carefully planned, enabling environment for the children to learn in enables the children to explore, play and discover, with staff alongside them listening, supporting and capturing this learning, without a need to plan ahead. She describes how planning 'in the moment' allows staff to respond to and help children develop immediately, for example if a child is trying to use a hammer, rather than planning in opportunities to do this next week, the staff support and teach the child in that moment to use the hammer, and this teaching/learning is put into the learning diary. I highly recommend her book, *The Nursery Year in Action*. She takes you through the year with many examples of how the approach works for their setting.

As adults we hold a lot of power, it is important that we provide children with clear boundaries and that we help children to feel safe and secure. However, we also need to allow children to find out, discover and explore for themselves. Sometimes, as adults we are tempted to over direct children, planning out everything for them and telling them how to do things. We need to find the balance between providing clear boundaries, along with the space for children to make mistakes and discover for themselves.

Stopping and listening

If we want children to be curious, inquisitive and creative, then we as adults need to model this to the children we are with and we need to show interest and curiosity in what the children are showing and telling us. When as adults we respond to children with curiosity and interest we are giving them a message that what they enjoy is important to us. In Chapter 2, I describe the need for adults to have time to slow down and really listen, to give time to children. One course I regularly deliver is about listening to children. An exercise I set in the training is to ask people to think back to a recent time when they stopped and listened to a child and when they saw the world in that moment through the child's eyes. This can be a challenging exercise; so often as parents, childcare workers, educators we are so busy doing, so busy telling, that we don't always stop and hear, stop and listen. In my experience, when we stop and listen, when we stop and show an interest, we can learn and discover so much from the child, about the child.

Co-adventuring together

I believe that the best early years staff and teachers are those who are able to let go of the control of being right and leading all the time and instead are able to allow the children to lead in their learning. Sometimes, as educators, we can have ideas in our head of what the children need to do and learn that week/month/term; I have observed some practitioners who can be quite rigid in their ideas. When you are trying to force a child to learn something that they are not interested in, you see a blankness develop in their eyes. In contrast when you discover something the child is interested in you see a light in their eyes, an excitement. It takes a gifted early years worker and educator who is able to let go of their agenda and follow the child's lead and recognise the learning that is happening through the child's discovery and playing. I recently observed one early years worker who had planned an activity involving weighing and measuring; the small group she was about to work with had just discovered a frog in the garden so, instead of insisting that the children came in to do her activity, as was planned, she followed the children's interest in and fascination with the frog. She joined the huddled group of children watching the frog, they spent around 30 minutes watching the frog, talking about how it moved, where it lived, what it ate. A couple of the children then chose to draw pictures of the frog, others went to look for books about frogs, another child chose to make a home for the frog out of sticks and grass. The adult was following the children's interest, she was showing her delight and interest in the frog; the children were asking questions to which she didn't know the answers and together they were learning and finding out. At that moment they didn't learn about measuring and weighing but they did learn about frogs and the environment, they learnt new words, they talked about how big the frog was and how high it could hop. Through the adult's ability to co-explore and discover with the children, by not rigidly sticking to her plan, the children and adult together had a rich learning experience.

Questions for practice and reflection

- Do you know what the current interests are of the children you work with or your own children?
- How do you include these interests in the provision you offer children?
- If you manage staff, do you encourage your staff to find out about or share an interest in what the children are interested in? Do you discuss this in supervision/team meetings?

Observing and listening to children

In early years practice, observations are an essential element of understanding what is happening for a child, how they are learning, what they are enjoying. There are many different types of observations. These can include a quick observation and noting down when a child has achieved something new, for example cutting with scissors for the first time, or a longer observation when an adult is watching the child for an extended period of time, noticing how they are playing, how they interact with others, any behaviours, what they are playing with. Fawcett (2009) explores the many different types of observations and explains how to use them. The key person role in early years settings is essential for adults to gain an in-depth knowledge of children through their observations; the key person approach in nurseries enables one person to build a loving, trusting relationship with the child, and to really learn about the individual child (Elfer, Goldschmied and Selleck 2003).

Provision for children's interests

Throughout the book, I have highlighted the importance of providing children with a rich learning environment. This includes adapting it to meet children's current fascination and interest. One reception class I worked with had a group of children who loved playing hairdressers, the teacher talked to the children about turning the home corner into a hairdressing salon, they discussed what they needed. They decided they needed chairs, towels, hair dryers, pretend scissors, rollers, mirrors, bottles of shampoo, hair spray and hair gel, and comics to look at while they were waiting. One of the children had an aunty who owned a hairdressing salon. This girl was able to provide some 'expert' knowledge; about hairdressers and the teacher spoke to the family and borrowed some things from the aunty's shop to use in the school salon. The children had a conversation before the salon was 'open' about using the scissors, why they had pretend scissors and how only adults were allowed to cut hair. The staff found the girl whose aunty was a hairdresser was often quiet and unconfident, but when it came to sharing her knowledge about hairdressers she was animated and was able to speak confidently about what she knew; the staff were delighted to see this confidence and discover this interest. The provision for children's interests can be as simple as ensuring you have a good selection of things that the children are currently fascinated by, for example toy dinosaurs if you have children who are keen on dinosaurs. There are items which you can keep in your setting which you may not have out as continuous provision, but you have in the cupboard for when children become interested. There are a few interests which appear year after year, examples are given in the box below.

Examples of interest provision

- dinosaurs – toys, books, dressing up clothes
- superhero characters – pictures, comics, toys, dressing up clothes
- princesses/make believe – princess and prince toys, unicorns, dragons, dressing up clothes, books
- bugs and insects – toys, books, magnifying glasses, butterfly growing kit.

With the list above I would add it is really important you don't fall into stereotypical categories of play, ensure there are female superhero characters as well as male, ensure you have alternative books on make believe rather than just the books where the princess needs rescuing by the princes. Some great examples are *Princess Daisy and the Dragon* by Steven Lenton (2015) and *The Worst Princess* by Anna Kemp (2012).

Provocation

In Reggio Emilia pre-schools, as mentioned in Chapter 5, staff often use a provocation. They will observe and note what the children are interested in and will bring something into the setting or take them out on a visit to act as a provocation. This provocation is a way of introducing a new element, a new possibility to the children, staff then observe the way the children respond. The provocation doesn't need to be big, for example for children who have a fascination with bugs the staff may bring in a wormery. By using provocations the adult is listening to the children, noticing their interests and helping to extend the children's knowledge and learning. The adult is actively engaging in creative thinking with the children; this engagement of adults in a creative way models to children ways of being excited, interested and curious.

Schemas

Schematic behaviours are a pattern a child repeats through their play, their actions and their language. Understanding schemas is a wonderful way to gain insight into a child's behaviour and interests. Some children have strong schematic interests, where they repeat certain actions or behaviours. My youngest daughter loved climbing; from around 15 months she would climb on everything she could. Sadly, I didn't know about schemas when she was small, if I had it would have given me a deeper knowledge and understanding about what she was doing and why; an understanding of the trajectory schematic interest that she had and I could have provided her with appropriate opportunities to explore this. A trajectory schema is one where children are fascinated by a type of movement, my daughter was fascinated by things that went up and by going up herself. I learnt about schemas when she was seven and was able to recognise her love of tree climbing fitted with this schema and we were able to enrol her into a climbing club;

she is now a very competent and able 17-year-old climber, who regularly climbs at the local climbing walls.

Schemas are patterns of behaviours which help children to make sense of their world, they can help children to learn new information and can extend their understanding (Athey 1990). Schematic interests can be seen when a child repeats a behaviour, for example a child who persistently throws, who will throw anything they can. One early years worker described to me a child in their nursery who threw everything he could; the staff were frustrated that he found it hard to obey the rule of no throwing, but when they learnt about the different types of schema, particularly the trajectory schema, they then understood what was happening for this child and were able to provide appropriate ways for the child to explore this, for example, through making paper planes and throwing them, throwing balls into a hoop and playing skittles. By better understanding the child and his interests the staff were able to support him in his learning.

When staff observe and notice a schematic interest, they are able to provide children with a variety of experiences that will extend their interest and learning (Nutbrown 2006). Identifying schemas is the easy part, the challenge is to then extend children's learning through their schematic interest (Athey 2013). As I have mentioned earlier, when we take the time to really observe, notice and listen to what the children are interested in, it helps us to have a deeper understanding of the children and to be able to support them better. We can then take the children's interests and provide them with increased and new opportunities to extend their interests. We need to use these interests to scaffold and extend the children's thinking and learning. In the example of the nursery identifying the child with a trajectory interest, they were able to use different resources and opportunities to extend his playing: the nursery staff were able to engage with him in conversations about throwing, distances he was throwing, what things are easier or harder to throw, they later went on to watch video footage of Olympic athletes throwing discus and shot-put.

Sharing knowledge of schemas with parents

As early years workers, by developing a knowledge and understanding about schemas, we are then able to share this with parents. Pen Green Children's Centre in Corby has been a pioneer in the way they have worked with parents to understand schemas. Whalley (2007) and her team have found working with parents to understand schemas has hugely benefited the parents and the children. A few children's centres I have worked with have developed information boards and leaflets for parents about schemas. I supported one nursery in developing their understanding of schemas, I delivered training for them and did some interviews with staff and parents a few months later. The staff felt that understanding schemas helped them to gain more insight into some of their children and enabled them to provide resources that really met the children's needs; they felt this had really enhanced their practice. I spoke with one parent who had a child with a rotational schema, the parent commented that the knowledge of schemas had helped her to understand why the child seemed so interested in wheels and clocks; she commented that she had begun to worry that her child's behaviour was strange when he would turn a car over and watch the wheels spin rather than push it along the ground. The staff helped her to understand the schematic interest her child had and how she could help extend this. The mum told me how she had recently bought him birthday presents to meet this interest, this included spinning sand toy wheels, windmills for the garden and how she had found tyres of different sizes to play with in the garden. She said they were the cheapest birthday presents she had bought him but that he was so happy and engaged for long periods of play with his presents.

Examples of the more common schemas

- transporting – moving toys, objects from one place to another, often filling pockets, baskets
- trajectory – interest in throwing, jumping, climbing, movement up and down
- connecting – enjoys joining things together, tying things together, linking objects, lining up objects
- rotational – loves things that go around, spin, twirl
- enveloping and containing – covering, hiding, wrapping things
- transformation – interested in how things change
- scattering – loves emptying and wiping.

Finding out more about schemas

If schemas are a new idea to you, I would highly recommend you seek out some of the excellent books and resources available on the subject. I particularly recommend *Threads of Thinking* by Cathy Nutbrown (2006), *Young Children Learning through Schemas* by Katey Mairs and the Pen Green Team, edited by Cath Arnold (2013). There is also an excellent video link by Cathy Nutbrown (2016) on the BBC CBeebies website. Additionally, the children's programme *All Twirlywoos* uses schemas in its play.

Questions for practice and reflection

- How often do you or your staff note down children's schematic interests in the children's learning diaries?
- How do you share your knowledge of schemas with parents?
- Are children's schemas on your list for discussion in supervision or team meetings?

If you are unfamiliar with schemas you may want to consider finding staff training to develop your staff's knowledge in this area.

References

Athey, C. (1990) *Extending Thought in Young Children.* London: Paul Chapman Publishing.

Athey, C. (2013) 'Beginning with the Theory about Schemas.' In K. Mairs and the Pen Green Team, edited by Cathy Arnold *Young Children Learning through Schemas.* Abingdon: Routledge.

DCSF (2008) *Practice Guidance for the Early Years Foundation Stage.* Available at www.foundationyears.org.uk/files/2011/10/EYFS_Practice_Guide1.pdf, accessed on 02/08/16.

Edwards, C., Gandini, L. and Forman, G. (1998) The *Hundred Languages of Children: The Reggio Emilia Approach – Advanced Reflections.* London: Alex Publishing.

Elfer, P., Goldschmied, E. and Selleck, D. (2003) *Key Persons in the Nursery.* Abingdon: David Fulton.

Ephgrave, A. (2015) *The Nursery Year in Action.* Abingdon: David Fulton.

Fawcett, M. (2009) *Learning through Child Observation.* London: Jessica Kingsley Publishers.

Kemp, A. (2012) *The Worst Princess.* London: Simon and Schuster.

Laevers, F. (2015) 'Making care and education more effective through wellbeing and involvement. An introduction to Experiential Education.' Available at vorming.Cego.be/images/downloads/Ond_DP_IntroductionExpEduc.pdf, accessed on 29/10/16.

Lenton, S. (2015) *Princess Daisy and the Dragon.* London: Nosy Crow.

Mairs, K. and the Pen Green Team, edited by Arnold, C. (2013) *Young Children Learning through Schemas.* Abingdon: Routledge.

Nutbrown, C. (2006) *Threads of Thinking.* London: Sage.

Nutbrown, C. (2016) 'Schemas: How children learn through play.' Available at www.bbc.co.uk/cbeebies/grownups/schemas, accessed on 17/08/16.

Whalley, M. (2007) *Involving Parents in their Children's Learning.* London: Sage.

Chapter 7

Adult Wellbeing

I think this is one of the most important chapters of this book and an area that is often neglected. If we are going to help the children we work with or look after to have good wellbeing, then we need to have good wellbeing ourselves. If the adults who are caring for or educating children are feeling low, unhappy or stressed out this will inevitably affect the children. Children do pick up on adults' emotions, feelings and attitudes.

Often at the end of term, when staff are really tired, worn out and feeling stressed, a common complaint is that the children are harder work. I believe there is often a coalition between the children's behaviour and the way the staff are feeling, children can be unsettled when the adults around them are unsettled. Children pick up on body language, atmosphere and unspoken messages; they don't just hear the words we say to them. The wellbeing project run by London Metropolitan University and the National Children's Bureau (Manning-Morton 2014) set a prerequisite of the staff. It stated that staff needed to have resilience and a good wellbeing; staff and managers needed to consider how the adults' self-esteem affected children, they recognised that staff self-esteem and wellbeing had an impact on children's wellbeing and self-esteem.

Poor staff wellbeing

I am seeing an increasing number of staff in schools and early years settings who are really stressed. I believe this is largely down to the proliferation of targets, changes and pressure from government onto schools as well as education and early years staff feeling undervalued. The low pay, heavy workload, lack of support from management and the pressure some staff receive from parents, all contribute to feeling undervalued for both school and early years staff (Simms 2006). Over the last year I have seen an increase in the number of teachers and TAs who have broken down in tears over the pressure, the intensity of the role and the workload. Richardson (2015) has reported on teaching unions' increasing concern about the poor wellbeing and stress of many teachers. If staff don't feel good about their work, if they don't feel valued, this will impact on their work with the children. It is vital that all staff looking after children feel equipped, supported and valued. It is essential that the staff are having their own needs looked after.

A survey of its members by one teaching union found that 76 per cent of teachers felt the job was having a negative effect on their mental health and were considering leaving the profession (Espinoza 2015). A survey of early years professionals around the same time found that 59 per cent were considering leaving their profession; reasons for this included stress from the increasing workload, poor pay and lack of support (Crown 2015). Government figures about the number of people who have time off from work due to work-related stress, anxiety and depression find that people working in education, health and social services experience more stress in their work place than most other jobs (Buckley 2015).

Secondary stress

An increasing number of early years settings and schools are finding that, as well as being put under extra pressure to achieve, they are finding a higher number of children they are working with have challenging behaviour or are experiencing difficult lives at home. An increasing number of children find the experience of being in nursery/school very stressful. This is difficult for staff; when staff are working with children who display challenging behaviour or are experiencing challenges at home, it is so important that they are given adequate support, supervision and training. In my nurture role I regularly see the stress that staff encounter while working with challenging children. To be frequently at the receiving end of a child screaming, throwing, biting, hitting, a child being highly distressed and unhappy, is very unsettling, challenging and distressing for staff. It takes a lot of calmness, perseverance, love for the child, and clear strategies and guidance for staff to be able to manage this. Some 1:1 staff encounter this daily and it does have an impact. Louise Bomber (2011) coined the term called 'secondary stress', this describes the situation where the stress the child is encountering and experiencing is picked up and experienced by the adult working with them. Bomber emphasises the importance of staff being aware of their own feelings at the start and end of each working day. Sometimes after working with a distressed or troubled child we can feel low and burdened, we have taken on these feelings from the child's experience. It is important that at the end of each day or each work session we have a chance to offload to someone and to express the challenges and the demands of the day. Bomber talks about creating rituals to signify the end of the day. One I particularly like is washing your hands at the end of the day and rubbing in scented hand cream. I love the symbolism of this act, of finishing work for the day but also of nurturing and caring for yourself. When working with distressed children, it is important both that the individual worker takes responsibility for caring for themselves, but also that the employer recognises the impact this work can have on staff and offers extra support, supervision and guidance.

Questions for practice and reflection

- How is your own wellbeing?
- When did you last feel overwhelmed/highly stressed/anxious?
- Who can you talk to about how you feel?
- What challenging behaviours do you feel impact most on you? In what way do they impact you?

The role of managers

It is essential that managers have good emotional intelligence themselves, this is crucial for managers to be able to support, lead and motivate their staff (Rodd 2006). Goleman (1996) suggests emotional intelligence enables you to understand and know your own feelings, understand and manage your emotions, be empathetic to others, be able to restore broken relationships and brokenness in yourself and be able to respond to others in an appropriate emotional way. If managers have good emotional intelligence themselves then they are in a better position to be able to support their staff. The Action for Happiness movement helps people look at their own wellbeing and their emotional intelligence, it suggests ways to help people improve their wellbeing. They have courses and ideas that you can use to help develop your wellbeing and emotional intelligence, their website is well worth exploring.[1]

Looking after our own wellbeing

There are some basic things we can all do to look after our own wellbeing. We talk to children about eating healthily, exercising, spending time outside, relaxing, getting enough sleep. We need to take these messages on board ourselves. We can all take responsibility for the food we eat, making sure we eat regularly and healthily. We tell children how important it is to eat breakfast each morning, but is this also a message we need to give to ourselves? We know that children are not able to concentrate, engage and learn without having

---

1   www.actionforhappiness.org

breakfast, it is the same for the adults looking after them. In my old office we had various breakfast cereals, bread and spreads available for staff. Quite a few of us would have breakfast and a coffee when we arrived at the office as, for many of us, the morning rush of getting our own children up and out of the house and getting ourselves ready for work meant that we would miss breakfast. Having this available in the office reminded us of the importance of eating and reminded us to take care of ourselves.

Taking exercise is something we often tell children they need to do. I know some nurseries that have mini gym equipment for children to play on; schools promote the importance of exercise, but often the staff don't do this for themselves. There are some settings that have linked staff to local zumba, dance and yoga classes. I know of a school that has a swimming pool on site and they allow the staff to use this at the beginning and end of the day. All the staff in one nursery did a sponsored run together to raise money for a cancer charity. Many schools and early years settings are good at making connections and signposting families to other agencies, but maybe we need to start making connections and signposting staff, for example persuading a local gym to give a discount to the nursery staff in return for advertising the gym with parents. We know that if staff are fit they are less likely to get ill.

Finding time to relax is an essential part of looking after our own wellbeing. This may be finding time to read for pleasure, listening to music, spending time with friends, gardening or walking, playing an instrument. The key is regularly taking time to relax. We are so quick to talk about how busy we are, but do we talk as much about the things we do that relax us, that we enjoy?

Questions for practice and reflection

- How could you eat more healthily?
- What kinds of exercise do you enjoy? How often are you able to make time for these?
- Could you improve the quality or quantity of your sleep?
- What do you find relaxing? How often are you able to make time for this?

Being kind to ourselves

Both as managers and workers we have a responsibility to be kind to ourselves. We cannot fully take care of the needs of our staff and the children if we are not taking care of ourselves. There are things that employers can do to look after the wellbeing of the work place which I discuss later in the chapter, but there are also things we can do as individuals to look after ourselves. I spend a lot of time in my nurture work asking staff what they are doing to be kind to themselves. At first this is often met with puzzled looks! I have particularly learnt through my nurture role that if we are looking after children who have high needs we really need to look after ourselves or we will burn out and become ill. When discussing this with staff I get them to think about things they can do that make them feel happy, these will be different for everyone. This is not about spending lots of money, doing big things, but it is about the small things that make a difference. One example I give staff is that I swim early each morning, I am a morning person so it works for me. This is my time; I find the rhythm of swimming comforting, I find it is a time when I can work things through in my mind or at other times just switch off and be in the moment and enjoy the rhythm of swimming. I have been doing this now for around five years and it has got me through some really tough emotional times. I know of staff who find knitting a really good switching off exercise, and have started knitting each day; another member of staff I work with got a dog and takes the dog for a walk when she gets back from work each day. It doesn't really matter what you do, as long as you are intentionally doing something for you that makes you feel happy. We cannot rely on others to provide us with happiness or self comfort. We need to learn to be self compassionate, to recognise when we are hurting, when we are finding life hard; at these times we need to learn to be kind to ourselves. Kristin Neff (2011) has written a fantastic book exploring this theme more.

Questions for practice and reflection

- How much time do you take to think about your own needs?
- What do you do weekly or daily that makes you feel happy?
- What do you do for yourself that helps improve your own wellbeing?
- How could you be more compassionate towards yourself?

Looking after your staff

As managers, it is so important to ask the question, 'How are you looking after your staff?' There is now a growing recognition of the need for managers to think about their staff wellbeing, as well as the wellbeing of the children. Tomsett (2013) suggests that headteachers (this is the same for nursery managers and children centre managers) need to prioritise their staff as highly as their students. He suggests you can't just say you put the children first, you need to meet both student and staff needs. If staff feel happy, cared for and respected, then they will go on to help the children feel happy, cared for and respected.

Examples of promoting wellbeing with staff

There are some innovative ideas that managers can put in place to look after their staff. Too often we hear of work places which don't look after their staff, there are many examples available. For this chapter I researched some good examples.

One friend told me she had seasonal affective disorder (SAD) one winter and her manager arranged for her to work in the senior manager's office that had a skylight; she was also encouraged to take short breaks in-between seeing the young clients she worked with and walk around the block to get some daylight and air. She felt without this she could have been off sick for a few weeks, but with this support she felt valued, cared for and respected. Another friend of mine is a manager in a children's centre. She makes homemade cakes for team meetings and in her team's supervision notes they have space for 'celebrations and wow moments' where they recognise what has gone well and what the individuals feel good about.

This can be so important, particularly when supervisions can be full of work requests, service issues and problems. I know of other work places that have paid for staff to attend an eight-week mindfulness programme and encourage staff to use mindful practice regularly themselves and with the children. In our old team we regularly had team away days, this always involved good food and often involved walking somewhere. It was an opportunity to be away from the work place, spend time with each other and spending time doing something we enjoyed together. This always helped us to feel valued and made us stronger as a team.

The environment

The environment you work in can have a big impact on staff wellbeing. Working in spaces which have natural light can really enhance wellbeing. Having a staff room with comfortable seats is vital in a school or early years setting– a space away from the children, a dedicated space for staff. This space should be uncluttered and comfortable and should be a space where staff feel they can sit and relax during their break. I know of nurseries that don't have a dedicated staff room. They instead have a spare room which staff use, but it is also used as a small group room with children. I do understand that space can be an issue for many settings, but the wellbeing of your staff is essential and providing them with an inviting, dedicated space is important. Ensuring staff take lunch breaks is very important; when I worked for a charity we were awful at taking lunch breaks, we often ate lunch at our desks or while driving to see the next client, which is a really unhealthy habit to develop. Some work places provide tea and coffee for their staff. This sounds like a small gesture but it is a way to help staff feel valued.

Supervision

For over 20 years I worked for a large children's charity. Monthly supervision was an embedded, essential part of the practice, and it has been in children's charities for many years. Monthly staff supervision is also an embedded part of the nurture outreach team I work with. Over the years I have been supervised, and I have also been a manager and supervised staff. Within early years practice, staff supervision is still relatively new though it was brought in as a requirement by the Department for Education (DFE) in 2012.

Supervision is about having the opportunity to talk through work, to discuss practice, to reflect on practice, to have support, encouragement, guidance and at times to be challenged (John 2012). Supervision should also be a place where a person can be honest about how they are feeling, what they are finding hard and where they can discuss questions they may have. The role of a supervisor is to listen, to guide, to support, to question and at times to lead. At the moment I have an amazing supervisor, an educational psychologist. I leave supervision feeling that I have been heard, that I have had the opportunity to reflect, question, discuss; but I also feel valued. My supervisor, Ruth, has a real talent for helping staff feel they are valued and for emotionally holding staff when times are hard. There have been times when I have sat in supervision and cried over cases, when I have felt overwhelmed at the difficulties of the lives of some of the children I work with, and Ruth has been able to hold that. When we work with people who are experiencing distress or feeling hopeless, it is easy to also feel distressed and hopeless. Karen John (2012) describes this as an emotional contagion, where we take on another's feelings. Supervision needs to offer time to reflect on how the work is making us feel and how we are responding. Every supervision I have had and have led has started with the question, 'How are you today?'; that simple question in itself can be very powerful, as long as the person answering it is honest and the person asking it really wants to know.

Supervision in schools is mostly unheard of and, as part of the nurture outreach role, we offer supervision to the staff who are working directly with the children, for example teachers and teaching assistants. It has been late coming into early years, but I think it has a really important role; unfortunately in some cases, supervision is a time when staff are told off, or are given a list of demands. Supervision needs to be a two-way listening and communication process, with both supervisor and supervisee having space to speak and be heard. I firmly believe supervision should become part of the school culture, so many staff I see now would really benefit from having regular supervision practice.

Questions for practice and reflection

- Do you have supervision in your work place? Is supervision a place where staff can be honest and open with their feelings and emotions?

- If you have supervision how do you ensure it is not just taken up with issues from work? Do you ask after your staff's wellbeing? Do you ask staff what they are doing to be kind to themselves?
- How do you encourage staff to be honest about how they are feeling and what is happening for them at work?

Ideas for supporting staff

Along with supervision, in the charity sector we also had annual staff appraisals. This is an opportunity to reflect back on the year, to think about what has gone well, what could have been done differently and what you want to do in the year ahead. This is an opportunity for staff to think about what their learning needs are and what areas they would like to develop in. This is a great opportunity for managers to hear their staff members' ideas and to be able to see ways they can support the staff in their roles. Sometimes this is about looking at training opportunities; as a trainer I am aware that training budgets are often being cut back, and I believe this is a real oversight and puts staff and organisations at a disadvantage. Training helps staff to develop and improve in their practice, it gives them opportunity to hear about new ideas and can help staff to feel valued and empowered in their job.

Another way to support staff is by encouraging a culture of reflective practice. Reflective practice enables staff to think about and reflect on their practice, ask questions and possibly change and develop their practice (Paige-Smith and Craft 2011). It is important to be in a safe space to be able to develop reflective practice, a place where staff feel it is ok to acknowledge when they could do things differently without fear of being penalised or judged. Reflective practice can be developed in supervision or team meetings and it encourages staff and settings to develop and enhance their practice, which is good for both staff and children.

Parents need to be kind to themselves

Finally in this chapter I also want to acknowledge the importance of parents being kind to themselves and taking care of their own wellbeing as well as the wellbeing of their family. We all know that parenting is the hardest of all jobs, and can also be the most rewarding. It is often said that parenting younger children is the hardest part, but I am not so sure about that. I now have a 17-year-old and 19-year-old, and of course the challenges are different, but there are still challenges across the ages and children of all ages still need parents to be present, interested and nurturing. Certainly, parenting young children is very tiring, with sleepless nights, the endless energy they have when they are awake, the need to always be aware of where they are, what they are doing and to answer the many, many questions. This can lead to parents feeling exhausted and drained. Just as staff looking after children need to look after themselves, so too do parents. It is worth spending time considering what you do to take care of yourself.

Ideas for improving wellbeing

- eating well
- exercising
- being creative – this might be through baking, drawing, playing an instrument, knitting, photography
- taking time to relax – having a hot bath with essential oils, reading a book, listening to music, watching a film
- taking up yoga or mindfulness – you don't need to attend a class, you can find online videos
- seeing friends
- laughing
- spending time outdoors.

If we can spend time being kind to ourselves, taking care of our own wellbeing then we are in a much better position to promote the wellbeing of the children we look after.

References

Bomber, L. (2011) *What About Me? Inclusive Strategies to Support Pupils with Attachment Difficulties Make It Through the School Day.* Kings Lynn: Worth Publishing.

Buckley, P. (2016) 'Work related Stress, Anxiety and Depression Statistics in Great Britain 2016.' Available at www.hse.gov.uk/statistics/causdis/stress/stress.pdf, accessed on 27/08/16.

Crown, H. (2015) 'Nursery workers consider leaving profession due to workload.' Available at www.nurseryworld.co.uk/nursery-world/news/1154397/nursery-workers-consider-leaving-profession-due-to-workload, accessed on 27/08/16.

DFE (2012) 'Overall Reforms to the 2012 EYFS Framework.' Available at www.foundationyears.org.uk/wp-content/uploads/2012/07/Overall-Reforms-to-the-2012-EYFS-Framework.pdf, accessed on 18/06/16.

Espinoza, J. (2015) '"Stress pushing teachers to leave profession", figures show.' *The Telegraph*, 18 March. Available at www.telegraph.co.uk/education/ educationnews/11480108/Stress-pushing-teachers-to-leave-profession- figures-show.html, accessed on 27/08/16.

Goleman, D. (1996) *Emotional Intelligence: Why It Can Matter More Than IQ*. London: Bloomsbury.

John, K. (2012) 'Supervision part 1: Equipped to lead.' *Nursery World*, May 25.

Manning-Morton, J. (2014) *Exploring Wellbeing in the Early Years*. Milton Keynes: Open University Press.

Neff, K. (2011) *Self Compassion*. New York: Harper Collins.

Paige-Smith, A. and Craft, A. (2011) *Developing Reflective Practice in the Early Years*. Milton Keynes: Open University Press.

Richardson, H. (2015) 'Stressed teachers being "reduced to tears".' Available at www.bbc.co.uk/news/education-34602720, accessed on 18/06/16.

Rodd, J. (2006) *Leadership in the Early Years*. Milton Keynes: Open University Press.

Simms, M. (2006) 'Recruitment and retention of early years and childcare practitioners in private day nurseries.' Available at http://tactyc.org.uk/pdfs/ Reflection-simms.pdf, accessed on 31/05/16.

Tomsett, J. (2013) 'How can headteachers and leaders promote staff well being?' Available at https://www.theguardian.com/teacher-network/teacher- blog/2013/jul/01/school-staff-wellbeing-headteacher-leaders, accessed on 29/10/16.

Conclusion

Throughout this book, I have explored the importance of why we need to ensure young children have good emotional health and wellbeing. We all know too many children and adults who are deeply sad and troubled; we also know that there are a growing number of children with poor wellbeing. I believe that every adult who comes into contact with a child has an opportunity to make a difference, to help that child feel good about themselves, just smiling, being curious and showing an interest can help the child feel good. I hope this book has given you practical ideas and suggestions that you can try out. I have been really privileged in my role as a nurture worker to use all these ideas with the four-year-olds I work with. There is a great joy in seeing the delight and pleasure in a child. I believe that working with young children is the best job in the world; sometimes it is hard but it can bring so much joy. I hope you enjoy promoting the emotional health and wellbeing of your children.

Index